Spiritual Exercises for

The hariyat

Book Two

Also by Harold Klemp

MAHANTA

This book has been authored by and published under the supervision of the Mahanta, the Living ECK Master, Sri Harold Klemp. It is the Word of ECK.

Spiritual Exercises for

The
Shariyat
Book Two

Harold Klemp

ECKANKAR
Minneapolis
www.Eckankar.org

Spiritual Exercises for the Shariyat, Book Two

Edited by Patrick Carroll, Joan Klemp, and Anthony Moore

Text photo (page xii) by Art Galbraith

Library of Congress Cataloging-in-Publication Data

Names: Klemp, Harold.
Title: Spiritual exercises for The Shariyat. Book two / Harold Klemp.
Description: Minneapolis : Eckankar, 2017.
Identifiers: LCCN 2017043518 | ISBN 9781570434525 (pbk. : alk. paper)
Subjects: LCSH: Spiritual life--Eckankar (Organization) | Eckankar
  (Organization)--Doctrines. | Twitchell, Paul, 1908-1971.
  Shariyat-Ki-Sugmad. Book 2.
Classification: LCC BP605.E3 K57363 2017 | DDC 299/.93--dc23 LC record
  available at https://lccn.loc.gov/2017043518

∞ This paper meets the requirements of ANSI/NISO Z39.48-1992 (Permanence of Paper).

The Spiritual Exercises of ECK are a treasure whose value we might overlook because of their simplicity. But they are your lifeline to the Word of God. The Mahanta has put this key to higher states of consciousness in your hand.

— Sri Harold Klemp

Note: This book of spiritual exercises is for use with *The Shariyat-Ki-Sugmad*, Book Two (abbreviated in the text as *SKS*, Bk. 2 or *"The Shariyat"*).

If you are using *The Shariyat-Ki-Sugmad*, Books One & Two, add 232 to find the correct page.

Contents

Sri Harold Klemp
The Mahanta, the Living ECK Master

Welcome

The Shariyat-Ki-Sugmad is the holy scripture of Eckankar.

It encompasses the wisdom and ecstatic knowledge of the spiritual worlds—your spiritual worlds. It contains the secrets that Soul needs to rise above the human passions that keep It in misery or despair. These scriptures cut through the illusions of temporal power.

So the books of the Shariyat-Ki-Sugmad lead Soul to wisdom, spiritual power, and freedom.

The Secret Doctrine

Only a small part of the whole Shariyat can be, or ever has been, put into the printed word. Most of it comes straight into the individual during the Spiritual Exercises of ECK as the Living Word, the Sound and Light of ECK.

You will find the whole of your experiences gathered and addressed, in some form or another, in the Shariyat-Ki-Sugmad. Yet 90 percent of what you learn about the Shariyat will be given in the other worlds by the Mahanta, the Inner Master.

The secret doctrine is the portion of the Shariyat-Ki-Sugmad that the Mahanta passes to the chela by means of the Spiritual Exercises of ECK.

This is the only authentic road to God, the one all spiritual travelers take to Mastership.

Open Your Spiritual Eye

I offer you these spiritual exercises for *The Shariyat,* Book Two to open your spiritual eyes and ears to the ECK Sound Current as It sweeps into the events of your daily life, dream worlds, and Soul Travel adventures.

Each exercise is akin to a visit to a Golden Wisdom Temple. It gives inner and outer training in how to look at daily life with your Spiritual Eye wide open. Many exercises include a little "homework" to expand your knowledge of the spiritual worlds as they relate to your personal unfoldment today.

Truth for You

Such a study of the Shariyat-Ki-Sugmad strengthens Soul and ignites Its curiosity to go further on Its journey home to God.

So read, contemplate, and listen for the Mahanta's words of truth for you. With your diligence, the Shariyat-Ki-Sugmad, Way of the Eternal, will open its secrets to you.

Harold

CHAPTER 1

The Eternal Dreamer of ECK

To Remember Soul's Dream

The Divine Dreamer sends out Its dreams to man via the Mahanta, the Living ECK Master in all Its worlds, to arouse individual Souls in their sleep state to seek once again the heavenly kingdom.

—*SKS*, Bk. 2, p. 1*

*I*n contemplation, sing *HU*, the ancient name for God, and invite the Master to more fully awaken you, Soul. Your experience may be one of energy, vibration, Sound, or Light.

Something you dream of as Soul brings an ecstasy of longing. Today, the Mahanta will heighten your awareness of this holy desire within you.

Watch for it.

* If you are using *The Shariyat-Ki-Sugmad*, Books One & Two, see note on page v about page numbers.

3

For an Experience of Divine Glory

> The opportunity comes again and again for every individual Soul who has spent time in this world. The Mahanta has been with each Soul time and again, but few accept him. They can neither see nor understand the divine glory which flows through him, which can take each into the heavenly worlds to live forever as Soul.
>
> —*SKS*, Bk. 2, p. 4

*S*ettle into a quiet place.

With eyes shut, picture a shimmering white screen in your inner vision. Softly chant the word *Mahanta* as *may-HON-tay* for a time. The Master's presence will first be felt in your heart. Let him open your Spiritual Eye and ears to the glory of a love beyond all measure.

* * *

This experience brings the need to acknowledge his blessing in your outer life in some way. Be a light of love to another Soul.

To Live in the Name of the Sugmad

Those who have had realization of Soul know that the Sugmad *is.* . . . It is understood only when the chela allows It to swallow him and digest him. When the chela lets himself surrender to It, It accepts him as a divine channel to be used in all the worlds of the universe.

—*SKS*, Bk. 2, pp. 6–7

*C*hoose a favorite passage from the ECK works that opens your mind and heart. Read it or recite it to yourself aloud. In contemplation, let its power— its essence— enter into the atoms of your being. See it transform you with its truth.

Then go about your day in the name of the Sugmad, with the glow of this knowing within you.

For Answers and Questions

The riddle of the question is forever plaguing the neophyte, for he never understands that no question can be put without an answer. Yet all questions are on the mental level; but the answers are always available before the question. In other words, there are always the answers to the problems of life, without the questions existing.

—*SKS*, Bk. 2, p. 10

*W*hat is your question of the heart?

You have an appointment to meet the Master on the inner planes in his study. He invites you to sit by him in a comfortable chair. Before you can pose your question or speak of your problem, he hands you a beautiful, sealed envelope.

Take your time. Sing *HU*, and examine the envelope, noting the manner in which it is sealed. Appreciate its beauty. There is a special way to open this envelope. You will discover this and its contents as you continue your experience.

To See Your Path of ECK

Once the chela steps onto the path of Eckankar, his karma begins to resolve and his reincarnations become fewer. When he is initiated, it means that never again will he have to return to this physical and material world. From the moment he steps upon the path of ECK, his spiritual life is under the protection and guidance of the Mahanta, the Living ECK Master.

—*SKS*, Bk. 2, p. 11

*I*n contemplation, imagine seeing the journey of Soul in the form of a rope laid out before you. The beginning sections of the rope display many knots and frayings, wear and weakening. Now observe the change in the quality of the rope where it marks your acceptance of the ECK path. It may become golden or gossamer or pulse with life.

The end of the rope, your future, reaches into the heart of God. Sing *HU* sweetly and softly, and see how the Master's love illuminates every next step of your journey.

*   *   *

In your day, look for an outer experience of this light of the Mahanta's love guiding your way. There will be more than one occasion.

7

The Disentanglement of Soul

In the value of emptiness must come the movement it permits, but the emptiness must come first. . . . This is why the ECK teachings concentrate quite frequently on the negativeness of self, on liberation of It from the so-called concepts of truth.

It proposes no idea, no description of what is to fill the void of the inner self, because the idea would exclude the greater truth which the inner self is seeking. Therefore, the practice of discipline must now enter into the scheme of liberation of Soul. This is the unfoldment and disentanglement of Soul from every identification It has had on every lower plane in the material or psychic worlds.

—*SKS*, Bk. 2, pp. 14–15

In the quiet of your inner being, feel a sacred space growing larger, brighter, sweeter with every HU you sing. It is a holy space for Soul and the Mahanta to explore the greater truth which the inner self is seeking. Sing *HU* or your secret word for twenty minutes or so.

*   *   *

Going forward, be prepared to let go of memories or the retelling of life stories that needlessly entangle Soul. Let the Inner Master help you clean out your inner closets.

There will be room for more love.

8

Seeing with the Eyes of Soul

When Soul leaves the physical body to journey into the far worlds, It usually does so through the Tisra Til, the Third Eye. It meets the Mahanta, the Living ECK Master after passing through the gate of the tenth opening, who escorts It into heavenly worlds where It experiences the joys and bliss of life.

—*SKS*, Bk. 2, p. 15

*W*ith your outer eyes still open, feel around with your spiritual senses for the location of your Spiritual Eye, the Tisra Til. It can be as simple as placing your attention inside your forehead, between the eyes, back an inch or so.

Now, with outer eyes shut, imagine an actual gate or gateway to an inner heaven. This is a doorway to God. Give it all your attention as you softly chant *Tisra Til.*

* * *

You may find yourself more aware of openings in your everyday life—open doors, windows, drawers, a break in the clouds, opportunities. These signs can remind you of your inner openness to the blessings of ECK.

To Hear the Music of Soul

In ECK there is the unmistakable tone of sincerity which makes the action which is not studied and contrived. Whosoever thinks and acts with a split mind rings like a cracked bell, one part standing aside to interfere with the other, to control, to condemn, or to admire.

—*SKS*, Bk. 2, p. 16

*S*hould you find yourself caught in a state of turmoil or in the grip of ego, stop and take a deep breath. Relax your inner tensions as you sing *HU*, the holy name of God. Do this three to five times.

Imagine your very being, Soul, ringing with a vibrant music like a bell intoning its sound. Listen for the waves of reverberations.

As you enjoy this cleansing sound you may begin to hear it with your outer ears.

Gain Freedom from the Past

The identification of the mind with its own image is paralyzing to the chela who seeks Self-Realization and God-Realization. This image is fixed from out of past lives, and finished as far as the ECKist is concerned. He wants nothing to do with this image, but it tries to react on him while he is doing the Spiritual Exercises of ECK.

—*SKS*, Bk. 2, pp. 17–18

*C*hoose a clean, quiet place for this appointment with the Inner Master. Begin by chanting *Akasha* (ah-KAHSH-ah) as a whisper. This is the primary Sound of every world within the universes of the Sugmad. It is the primal matter force that enters into the composition of all beings and things in life.

The Mahanta will invite you to explore an inner landscape fashioned of the living Light and Sound. It shimmers with your true potential and God's love for Soul.

* * *

In your daily life, there will be opportunities to go beyond fixed patterns. Some will appear as common, inconsequential choices. You will profit from being aware of these doors to greater freedom.

11

For the Living Experience

The Mahanta, the Living ECK Master knows at all times what goes on, and the ECKist should realize by now that he is never alone in his life regardless of whatever he is doing or wherever he might be. He should know by the living experience that the presence of the Mahanta is known through seeing and feeling. That this is reality and no one can take this from him.

—*SKS*, Bk. 2, pp. 19–20

 $\mathcal{C}$ hoose an image of the Master that especially opens your heart. As you contemplate his gaze, you may feel a welcome stillness of the mind.

Keeping your eyes open, sing Z for several moments, closing your eyes when you are ready to. Feel the Master's smile in your heart. The light in his eyes shines for you.

*   *   *

At some point in your day, you will suddenly be aware of the Master in your thoughts, in your being. This treasure is yours alone.

To Heal an Error

All life becomes a realization that the Mahanta is always present, and that the ECK makes life a joy to live. If the chela errs at any time there should be little need for discouragement, but one of joy, for he can now compare the errors with the joys of his life.

—*SKS*, Bk. 2, p. 20

*S*ing *H-U* one letter at a time aloud for several minutes. After a bit, you will feel your body come into harmony with this rhythm.

In your Spiritual Eye, imagine meeting the Mahanta by an inner fountain of Light and Sound. You may feel fountain spray upon your atoms or hear the waters rush like the life force in your veins.

Let this purifying action bring you joy.

*   *   *

Should you be distracted from the present moment by regret or remorse, practice the gift of true surrender. Give the situation to the ECK by saying with all your love and trust, "May the blessings be."

Know that the ECK will use the situation for the spiritual benefit of all.

CHAPTER 2

ECK, the Everlasting Gospel

To Realize Soul

When the eternal individuality of things is recognized, Soul is in abeyance. The infinite in all life
is at one with the infinite in man. In this sense the
Sugmad becomes as man is, that man may be as
It is.

—*SKS*, Bk. 2, p. 22

ead this passage aloud to yourself, slowly, let-
ting each phrase reach into your inner bodies. Then
chant *HU* for several minutes.

Imagine yourself, Soul, as a body of golden light.
The Master's love for you pulses in the center of this
light. Let this love and light expand until you are without beginning or ending.

You will find more to this experience. It's up to you.

Striving for Freedom

The state of perfection is a condition of free unfoldment of identity, through the continual annihilation of the lower self in all its forms by Soul, as It travels through all the planes to reach the heavenly worlds. To explore the vision of individuality, which strives to be free from the chains of the lower world and Kal, is that which inevitably allows passage from the human consciousness state to the individuality of Soul.

—*SKS*, Bk. 2, p. 23

*W*hat spiritual quality do you have a desire to exemplify in your daily living? Compassion? Silence? Selflessness? You are invited to a Satsang class led by the Inner Master on your chosen quality. It is being held on the inner planes in a spacious, circular room with a high domed ceiling.

There's a special seat waiting for you. Chant the word *Satsang* as you go into contemplation and join the class.

* * *

Over time, practicing the spiritual quality you focused on will bring you an unexpected freedom in some area of your life, inwardly or outwardly. It will be a joy to Soul.

To Live from the Heart

Man's personal experience of liberation is the liberation of his neighbor, the community in which he dwells, his state and nation, and eventually the world. His liberation eventually reaches out and touches all things in life; for he is linked with the very essence of things within the universes of God. He cannot expect to have any experience in life, be it negative or positive, and not have it affect the next person.

—*SKS*, Bk. 2, p. 24

*I*n contemplation, imagine you can view the very heart of your being. It is the ECK, Soul, a spark of God. What do you see?

*   *   *

This one day, act as if others will see or feel what you perceived in your contemplation. Let the heart of your being shine as a lighthouse to others. Do this in the name of the Mahanta, as you continue with your day.

For a New Approach

Man must not think that if he asks the Mahanta's help while facing a serious problem that the Sugmad will remove it to suit man's desires. It works in a different way; the problem itself may remain, but man's approach to it, his understanding of it, will change as a result of his petition. Whereas it may seem a very difficult, even insurmountable battle to face, man will be given the help needed in resolving it.

—*SKS*, Bk. 2, p. 25

When you face hardship of any kind, prepare yourself to receive the Master's help in the following way.

In a private, quiet place go into contemplation chanting the word *HUK*. It is a word for the inaccessible plane, the Agam Lok. As you chant, relax deeply and open yourself to a new inflow of Light and Sound. This will bathe you in renewal and rebirth. It reaches beyond the mind.

Invest twenty minutes in this exercise if you can.

*   *   *

Watch for the experiences, viewpoints, dreams, or other forms of guidance the Mahanta provides to help you take a new approach to your problem.

Your trust in him lights the way.

Making Yourself Free

Man's rebellion against Kal is natural. He is involved with those many things which enslave him, like government, taxes, business, the law, religion, education, media, law enforcement, and body chemistry which is known as medicine. He battles to untangle himself from these forces of the Kal Niranjan, but few have any success until they come into the presence of the Mahanta, the Living ECK Master, who will raise them above all these things. It is then that they can become detached from these aspects and traps of the Kal, and make themselves free.

—*SKS*, Bk. 2, p. 25

ing the words *Maha Nada* (MAH-hah NAH-dah) aloud for several minutes. This sound is another name for the great music of the Life Current. After a time, chant it silently.

On the inner planes, watch as the Mahanta channels this living music into your heart and being.

* * *

Be aware of moments in your life where you are guided to make a change in thinking patterns or emotional reactions. You may first notice a discomfort as you lift beyond the usual and reach for the freedom of Soul.

To Become a Greater Being

The great social lie is that he must be like others within the human race. He is born, sleeps, works, excretes, and reproduces. This is the basis of the life in which he lives in slavery to the human needs of his body. But he rises above this in the Atma Sarup and becomes a greater being in the eyes of the Sugmad, because he no longer needs the social lie.

—*SKS*, Bk. 2, pp. 27–28

*I*magine you are in the Temple of ECK and you see an ECK Master holding open the door of a golden elevator. He invites you to enter.

As the doors close and you begin to rise, notice how the inside of the elevator changes. It becomes larger, more spacious, and with each passing floor you can feel the wind speed of your ascent. Your body becomes finer and sparkles with Light and Sound. When you reach your destination the door opens.

Continue with your experience.

*   *   *

This very day, life will bring you the chance to re-member who and what you truly are through some choice you will make. Behind the scenes, the Master is holding open the elevator door.

Choose wisely.

For the Burning Love of God

If a chela is in the act of Soul Travel and sees that someone on one of the lower planes is in need of his help, he should leave his journey and go serve that person. The very act of entering into the heavenly worlds, via Soul Travel, brings with it an intense and burning love of the Sugmad which must meet the need of the overflow into the world for all fellow men and creatures, and this must show itself in deeds of charity, mercy, and self-sacrifice, and not merely in words.

—*SKS*, Bk. 2, pp. 33–34

In a whisper only you can hear, chant *SUGMAD* for several minutes. Listen in your heart. It is the name of the Ages and the Infinite. Look to experience the peace beyond all understanding. This love is food for Soul, for you.

* * *

Watch for the chance to share the love of the Sugmad with any person or being hungry for your deeds of charity, mercy, self-sacrifice. Then act.

Look and listen for your blessing.

To Receive Truth

Only the prophet knows and hears the Voice of the Sugmad. The prophet is the Mahanta, the Living ECK Master; he alone can give the truth. He awakens the faith and Spirit in every individual with whom he comes in contact, whether it is in the flesh or the Atma Sarup. He speaks with the pure essence of the ECK. This is the ultimate purity and unity, the all-embracing wholeness, the quintessence of truth.

—*SKS*, Bk. 2, pp. 35–36

*W*ith eyes shut, take three deep breaths and sing Z *Mahanta* for several minutes. As your Spiritual Eye opens, expect to feel the presence of the Mahanta in some way right for you.

You may experience a sweet, profound love, see or sense a glowing light, or hear a sound vibrating within your being. The Mahanta is speaking to you.

*   *   *

In your daily life you may find you are more open-minded to receiving new ideas and deciding what is true for you. Give special notice to what catches your attention.

24

The Two Doors of Soul

Soul has two aspects. The metaphor of the two doors of Soul means that It can look outward into the space-time of the Pinda world, the world of becoming; or It can look inward into the worlds of Sat Desha, the pure spiritual worlds of God, the world of being. Entering into the true Soul consciousness, the chela empties himself of all multiplicity, the things of the physical and psychic worlds. This is the apex of Soul consciousness for then It may behold with clarity what the Sugmad wishes for It to know, see, and do in this dazzling world.

—SKS, Bk. 2, p. 36

*U*sing your divine imagination, see yourself meeting the Mahanta in an endless landscape of sparkling golden sand. A sweet, musical wind swirls gently about you.

Begin to chant the word *Desha*. You may feel an effervescent light upon your body. This will be highly enjoyable. Let the Mahanta show you what is right for you to see in this high world of being.

*　　*　　*

This experience brings greater awareness. As you face a question or challenge, let the Inner Master show you the two doors of Soul. Is your answer one of becoming, or one of being?

Either way, his love is with you.

For Freedom and Rebirth

If he feels dissatisfied somehow with this life, if there is something in his ordinary way of living that deprives him of freedom in its most sanctified sense, he must endeavor to find a way somewhere which gives him a sense of finality and contentment. ECK will do this for all concerned, and It assures one of the acquirement of a new point of view in which life assumes a fresher, deeper, and more satisfying aspect.

—*SKS*, Bk. 2, pp. 36–37

*B*egin by singing *HU* or your secret word. Imagine a great purifying fire of renewal consuming all that is old, lifeless, dry, and empty in your life. All is consumed in a white flame of the ECK Current—a sight to behold. Stand back and appreciate its power.

As the fire dies down, you see that in its place runs a fresh, cool stream of singing waters.

These waters can be used to nurture the rebirth you desire. Ask the Mahanta to show you his ways.

*　　*　　*

This day, the ECK will show you one change, one thing you are ready to give up to gain more freedom in your life. Look for this divine invitation.

A Soul Travel Experience

To be released from this restriction the chela must become a Soul traveler who moves into that arena where all things are intensely exalted. When one has experienced the ECKshar, a hut may become a splendid palace because of the sharp increase of awareness in the spiritual sense. While on the other hand, without the ECKshar, the splendid palace may be that which looks dull and uninspiring, like the hut to the outer senses.

—*SKS*, Bk. 2, p. 39

*I*s there something in your life that appears dull and uninspiring—a job, relationship, or situation? Sing the word *ECKshar* in contemplation for several moments.

Imagine yourself meeting the Master in a palace of unspeakable beauty. As you tour the rooms and grounds you may see or experience things that seem familiar. Outside in the brilliant sunlight, the Master takes you to a mirror which reflects the love of God. He instructs you to look into the mirror. Continue with your experience.

*   *   *

Take this freedom and joy of being into your daily life. Look again at your challenge. Whenever you need, you can remember what you saw in the mirror.

CHAPTER 3

&

The Four Zoas of Eckankar

Contemplation on the ECK

This spiritual contemplation of the ECK is the greatest resource of strength that the chela may have for himself. It is the ultimate lift for him and will help him where intellect and all other things have failed him.

—*SKS*, Bk. 2, p. 43

*S*ing *E-C-K* one letter at a time for as long as you like. It may become a melody, even a familiar one. Let the song find its own way as it arises from your inner being. After a time, be silent and imagine your very atoms singing with this word.

It's a way for Soul to come into harmony with the divine intelligence.

*   *   *

When you need help of any kind, remember this melody of your inner being.

31

The Four Requirements

The ECKist knows that he must steer himself on the path to God, and that not even the Mahanta, the Living ECK Master can give him help unless he works in accordance with the laws of Eckankar. What he requires is restraint, compassion, self-awareness, and wisdom.

—*SKS*, Bk. 2, p. 44

*M*ake an appointment with the Mahanta for personal training to master each requirement given above.

Choose one quality at a time to spend a day focusing on. Let the Master show you how that particular quality holds a secret to take you further on the path to God. Your insights may come in contemplation and will certainly show up in the events of your day.

Invest the time to reflect on your experiences.

The One Single Deed

For all must know that none shall achieve absorption into the heart of the Sugmad by prayer alone, nor by good deeds, nor the motives of charity and love for one another. But not alone will any of these take Soul into the heart of the Sugmad. Yet if anything can give help, it is detachment from materialism, the act itself, where one single deed or action is worth more than a thousand good thoughts and can bring about that which takes Soul into the heavenly world.

—*SKS*, Bk. 2, p. 45

Silently sing the word *vairag* with your attention fully on your Spiritual Eye. Let this charged sound echo within you.

* * *

The Mahanta will speak to you in the secret language throughout your day, lighting up chances for you to gain strength in detachment. Follow through with one of these opportunities.

This act links you with the heart of the Sugmad.

To Win the Battle

The inner battle between life and physical death usually lies deeply hidden in man, and the struggle frequently shows itself, usually in the most paradoxical way.

Some of these paradoxical ways are the fear of failure in many things, or perhaps of physical danger, such as walking across a bridge over a high canyon. Another is social failure, in which one loses all his material goods or has a great social downfall.

—*SKS*, Bk. 2, p. 47

Close your eyes and sing *HU* eight to ten times. Picture yourself meeting the Master in a majestic mountain range. You stand with him, overlooking the vast expanse between where you now stand and yet another peak in the distance.

Spanning this space is a narrow footbridge with no handrails. It is up to you to begin the journey across the divide.

You will have several experiences as you cross this bridge. They are the Master's way of speaking to your underlying fears. Note them well.

The Master's Love

He must always remember that the Mahanta, the Living ECK Master is not the one to tell him of his inner experiences, nor whether the ECK Master has appeared to him. But he must know this with a faith that is beyond anything that he has ever experienced and, therefore, it will stay with him.

—*SKS*, Bk. 2, p. 51

*C*hoose a favorite image of the Master, the one that most touches your heart. Look into his eyes, and see him looking at you—into you—with pure love and delight. This is a truth for Soul to accept.

What will you do with this gift? Your day will bring you an opportunity to look at someone with love, compassion, mercy. Don't miss it.

Perceptions for Self-Realization

The four Zoas (laws) of Eckankar for the Mahdis, the initiate of the Fifth Circle, are . . .

—*SKS*, Bk. 2, p. 51

*T*urn to page 51 in *The Shariyat*, and read these Zoas carefully. Invite the Mahanta to open your heart and Spiritual Eye to new heights of perception as you contemplate upon your reading.

The true power of each of these Zoas is often beyond the mind yet nonetheless precious to Soul.

Over time, your realization will deepen, bringing gratitude and great upliftment.

The Law of Love

> The Mahdis shall have humility, love, and freedom from all bonds of creeds. He shall be free from the laws of karma which snare him with boastfulness and vanity. He shall have love for all people and all creatures of the Sugmad.
>
> —*SKS*, Bk. 2, p. 52

*G*ently chant the word *dinta*, a spiritual word for humility. Imagine the gaze of the Inner Master—love and mercy shining in his eyes. Let it purify your heart with its warmth, power, and joy.

*   *   *

You will find having an attitude of humility in a certain situation will bring you freedom from a burden of the past. The Master will, in some special way, alert you to this gift.

To Surrender Limitation

> The purpose of the Living ECK Master is there-
> fore to give all he possesses in return to the chela
> for giving all that he has.
>
> —*SKS*, Bk. 2, p. 53

*M*ake a list on paper of what you wish to surrender of yourself to the Mahanta.

First list the things that come to mind easily. Then
go into light contemplation as you chant *HU*. Let the
Master show you the subtler attachments that place
limits upon the light of Soul. These may be things you
would never think of as limitations. Be open.

See yourself releasing these identities to the Mahanta.

*   *   *

In a way you will recognize, you will perceive the
presence of the Master in a clearer, more certain light.
It will light your day.

For the Secret Doctrine

Mental acrobatics or tortuous, complicated philosophical gymnastics are not required in ECK. Nor is there any necessity for a chela to pore for hours over a page or an extract from some book or writings in order to grasp what the author means. The ECKist needs none of this. . . . Truth always expresses itself with the greatest simplicity.

—*SKS*, Bk. 2, p. 53

Open to page 53 of *The Shariyat-Ki-Sugmad*, Book Two, and find the four principles given there. Read them aloud slowly, and listen carefully to your voice as you say each word. Do this three times. Then shut your eyes and go into contemplation.

The Mahanta will pass on a portion of the Shariyat—the secret doctrine—directly to Soul.

* * *

If there has been a question or problem bothering you, look for the simplest answer, the simplest reason. Start there.

For the Inner Association of the Master

Spirituality, therefore, cannot be taught, but it must be caught. Once one has learned the secrets of ECK at the feet of the Mahanta and is enlivened with the life impulses received from him, it is no longer essential to be in constant physical association with him. The chela will have inner association with him anywhere and everywhere.

—*SKS*, Bk. 2, pp. 53–54

*S*ing *HU* or your secret word for several minutes. Reach into your heart, where your desire for God, for all things sacred and good, pulses with life. Contemplate this presence of the Mahanta within you.

*　　*　　*

Hold conversations with the Mahanta as you go about your day. Speak about everyday things on your mind, ask questions, and enjoy the company of your dearest friend.

Union with the Sound Current

Sat means true or unchangeable, and sang means union. Therefore, union with that which is pure and imperishable is Satsang, . . . going in and making contact with the ECK Sound Current is Satsang. The union of one with the Living ECK Master is Satsang.

—SKS, Bk. 2, p. 54

Begin to chant a favorite ECK word as you go into contemplation. Imagine you are having a Satsang experience with this sound.

This will be boundless, holy, personal, true.

*   *   *

Look for openings to have a waking Satsang experience. It could be in conversation with a seeker, an experience of nature, or a special awareness as you perform some simple duty in your day. You will find it a blessing.

The Path to Success

> The truth lies in the fact that before unfolding any faculty or powers which man has within himself and doesn't know about, he must acquire and learn about faculties and powers which he has and never uses. This is the missing link and the most important point in the spiritual evolution of man.
>
> —*SKS*, Bk. 2, p. 61

*I*s there a challenge in your life impossible to solve? There is always a way to be in harmony with the ECK. Take this as your first priority.

Go to the index of *The Shariyat* or any other ECK book and look up *God-Realization*. Choose two or three passages to research. Then take your findings into contemplation. The Mahanta can show you a path to success.

* * *

This exercise will stretch you. You may find you see every event more clearly for a time.

Then, get ready for more stretching.

CHAPTER 4

&

The Shab, the Lover of Life

For True Survival

The love of life begins with the descent of Soul into this physical universe. It is the great survival factor which all Souls have, some greater than others; but it is always there, instilled in each so deeply that often it must be uncovered by the Mahanta, the Living ECK Master to give the seeker something creative in his life.

—*SKS*, Bk. 2, p. 63

*T*ake a few deep breaths and sing *HU* for several moments. The Master's love for you glows in your heart, refreshing your love for life. This two-way flow may appear as a fountain, a vibrating circle of Light, or even as two drops of water beading together. Let the Inner Master create a vision for you.

*   *   *

In your day, remember this love as you use your creativity to resolve conflicts from a spiritual perspective.

45

For Greater Spiritual Character

All the virtues of the ethical system which man must live by are not forgotten in these books of the Shariyat-Ki-Sugmad: charity, kindness, self-control in speech and action, chastity, protection of the weak, benevolence toward the lowly, deference toward superiors, and respect for the property of others, even to the smallest details, will be found expressed in admirable language.

—*SKS*, Bk. 2, p. 65

*W*hich of the virtues given above could polish your spiritual character at this time? Sing *HU* or your secret word inwardly as you look them over again. Choose one.

With love for yourself as a child of ECK, compose a statement that affirms your desire for this quality—a statement to write fifteen times a day as a spiritual exercise. Make it something that brings joy and a light to your being to reflect on.

You are looking into a spiritual mirror, so choose your words with care.

To Stand for God

The upright man, that is the man who has all his life striven to find the ECK and to give ear to Its voice, when liberated from the body does not merely become the ECK, but he becomes the eternal vehicle who acts as the channel for the Voice of God.

—*SKS*, Bk. 2, p. 66

*W*ith eyes shut, chant the word *Qualima* (kwah-LEE-mah) for 10–20 minutes. This is another name for absolute truth, the divine melody, the music of the spheres. The ECK Itself. Open your spiritual ears to this sound.

*　　*　　*

In the course of your day, you will have an opportunity to stand taller spiritually. This is a gift from the Master to you.

Your Role in the Hierarchy

The Sugmad takes control of all life through Its counterparts such as the ECK; the lords, rulers, and governors of each plane; the ECK Masters of the Vairagi; and those beings who are the Co-workers of Itself. All these work through and with the Mahanta, the Living ECK Master, whose spiritual body is stationed on every plane within the universe.

—*SKS*, Bk. 2, p. 67

*S*ing *Vairagi* for several minutes. You are invited to a gathering on the inner planes where the Master and several ECK Adepts are instructing volunteers on how to help with a project. Take your seat. There will be a role for you. You may or may not remember what it is when you come out of this contemplation.

* * *

As a chela of the Mahanta, you are working within the spiritual hierarchy every moment of your day. Sing or say the word *Vairagi* whenever you want to be more aware of this. Your disciplines will be key.

For Self-Control

He is a machine which, in the right circumstances and with the right treatment, can know he is a machine; and having fully realized this, he may find ways to cease to be a machine. An individual traveling the path of ECK soon learns that he is more than this, that he is a spiritual being with full control over his emotions and desires.

—SKS, Bk. 2, p. 69

*S*hould you feel an unbalancing desire or emotion, imagine a field of protection around yourself. It may be an impenetrable light, a barrier of sound, or a reflective shield.

Look also for a specific action you can take to protect your reflexes from emotional outbursts—counting to ten, repeating a favorite ECK song lyric, or imagining yourself zipping up your aura.

Look forward to an opportunity to exercise this freedom. There is more to gain.

Shariyat Wisdom

> If he allows himself to be guided by the Living ECK Master, there is, of course, the opportunity to study the Shariyat-Ki-Sugmad directly in certain Temples of Golden Wisdom in the other worlds.
>
> —*SKS*, Bk. 2, p. 71

*C*lose your eyes and chant *Shariyat* for five minutes or so, then go into silent contemplation.

See yourself approaching a golden volume of the Shariyat set on a lectern in a sanctuary. At first, letters, words, and images rapidly shift on the page of these living sacred scriptures. The motion begins to slow, and a language you have never seen appears on the page. Yet it speaks to you. The Mahanta stretches out his hand and touches your Spiritual Eye with his finger. Accept this Golden Wisdom in the center of your being.

*   *   *

In your everyday life, you may find you have a desire to listen more carefully to others. You may have greater understanding of events in your life and the motives of others.

This is the wisdom of the Shariyat speaking to you.

To Listen and Understand

The chelas, having been raised in different environments and having varied attitudes, fixed opinions, and ideas about religions, do not understand and cannot open themselves to the words and teachings of the Living ECK Master. Mainly, they do not understand that he is speaking to each on the Soul level, that he knows and understands that each is immortal within the limits of the universes of God and, therefore, he speaks to each in this manner.

This can be said to be the new language, but so few understand it.

—*SKS*, Bk. 2, pp. 75–76

*I*magine that you are sitting on a grassy hill, just before sunrise, in the company of the Master. The horizon appears breathtakingly infinite, and the sky glows with celestial bodies that shine like jewels.

Look about you, as you silently listen with the Master to the Song of the Universe—the ECK.

*   *   *

As you go on with your day, there will be a particular encounter or event that catches your full attention. Through this, the Mahanta is speaking to you on the Soul level.

What do you hear?

To Live in the Name of the Mahanta

Nearly all commandments say, Do right, but few know what is being said here except the Living ECK Master, who gets to the heart of the problem. Most religions, instead, write down their laws in a book and assign penalties for their violations. Nearly all of them sum up the matter by saying, Do the will of God.

—*SKS*, Bk. 2, p. 78

*I*n a quiet place, sing Z or *Wah* Z for several minutes. Dedicate your thoughts, deeds, emotions, and even desires as channels for the Mahanta's love.

You may become aware of his presence as a shower of sparkling light settling on your heart and Spiritual Eye or feel the warmth of his love like a soothing golden honey.

* * *

Living in the name of the Mahanta will be a blessing of wisdom and spiritual freedom.

A Clearer View

Nothing can be morally good if a single individual has to be sacrificed to gain it. Therefore, the cure for evil is the unobstructed Sound and Light. When this occurs, as in the case of the Living ECK Master, then all darkness and evil vanishes, as the night disappears when the sun rises.

—*SKS*, Bk. 2, p. 79

*C*onsider an obstacle in your life that has resisted all efforts to resolve it. In contemplation, sing the word *vihara* (vee-HAH-rah), the dwelling place of consciousness. The Inner Master will show you what this signifies.

Some aspect of this obstacle is bringing the promise of greater Light and Sound into your world. Find gratitude for this spiritual fact.

Your gratitude will invite a clearer view of your situation.

The Golden Coin

It is love and love only which will admit the seeker to all the heavenly worlds, for it is the golden coin which must be presented when entering the high regions of Spirit. Nothing else will do because the doors of these worlds will not open for any other reason.

—*SKS*, Bk. 2, p. 80

*S*pend a few minutes contemplating this passage.

Today the Mahanta will offer you profound and humble opportunities to earn this golden coin. They may be subtle, easy to overlook, or difficult to accept. They may even be warm and joyful.

Use the word *Shab* in your contemplation and throughout your day to keep your heart open and at the ready.

The Pure Act of Love

The pure act of love lies mainly in the personal mantra of the ECK initiate. It can be described mainly as a sacred prayer-song which, when repeatedly chanted over a long period of time, gradually converts the devotee into a living center of spiritual vibration which is attuned to some other center of vibration vastly more powerful than his own.

—*SKS*, Bk. 2, pp. 81–82

*A*s you chant *HU* or your secret word, experience yourself as a living center of spiritual vibration attuning to the song of the Sugmad. The Mahanta may give you an insight to change the tone, cadence, or some other aspect of your chanting.

See how this attunement brings more life, energy, and ECK direction to your being. Continue for twenty minutes or more.

*   *   *

Going forward, you may find you have an easy access to the penetrating vision of Soul. Give space for this in your thoughts and feelings before you speak or react to others.

The Word of Change

Few, if any, will ever learn what has happened, but the mantra built up by the ECKist either individually or collectively will bring about a change in the worlds; first, that of man and then that of the spiritual heavens where necessary.

—*SKS*, Bk. 2, p. 83

*P*repare by shutting your eyes and taking a few long, deep breaths. Sing *HU* or your secret word, and let the Master show you how your love for the Sound Current becomes a vehicle for God's will in your life and the world.

Sing in the name of the Sugmad.

CHAPTER 5

Gakko, the World of Being

Taking the Next Step

It is known that having attained the stature of an ECK Master, it is found that there yet lies beyond this higher and even higher stages of spiritual evolution. One of the three truths of ECK is that Soul is immortal, and Its future is the future of a thing whose growth and splendor has no limits.

—*SKS*, Bk. 2, pp. 85–86

When facing a limitation in your inner or outer life, close your eyes and sing, "May the blessings be" for several minutes. Imagine unmanifested blessings of Light and Sound are raining into your life from the Ocean of Love and Mercy.

* * *

Your acceptance of unknown blessings invites new possibilities. Look for how the ECK will lead you forward.

Be hungry to take the next step.

Preparing Your Future

The ECK Masters, along with yet higher entities, form an inner, esoteric ring. In Eckankar they are known as the Adepts of the Vairagi. Their existence has been known to mystics and occultists in every age, and they are the "just men" in the sacred scriptures of the West made perfect.

—*SKS*, Bk. 2, p. 87

*W*hat qualities would you expect to see in an Adept of the Vairagi, an ECK Master?

As you contemplate your answer, the Mahanta will bring certain attributes to light. Write them down. These attributes are the very ones you are in the process of refining today.

The Inner Master may show you this connection in your dreams, through the conflicts of living, or by opening your Spiritual Eye at special moments in your daily life.

The Alchemy of Transmutation

He realizes intuitively that the Knower, which is the Sugmad, and all objects of knowledge, or all knowing, are inseparably linked together; and simultaneously, with this realization is born what is known as the great symbol which signifies his spiritual illumination. This symbol is known to every ECKist as the ECK, the "E...C...K," either sung or placed in the mind as a symbol. It purges from the mind the dross of ignorance, and the human is transmuted into the divine by the spiritual alchemy of Eckankar.

—*SKS*, Bk. 2, p. 89

In contemplation, try either or both of the techniques given in this passage. You may perceive a fine vibration cleansing your inner bodies, subtly but thoroughly. Let the Light of ECK and the Sound of ECK sing Its way into the heart of your being.

*   *   *

Consciously invite change and refinement into your life. Look for the opportunities the Master will offer you today, and you will benefit.

To Be Rhythmic with Soul

The chela is directed to go to a place like an isolated room or an outdoor place where he might not be disturbed, such as a garden, an orchard, or a hilltop, in which no human sounds can be heard. Here one attunes the body with the mind which becomes rhythmic with Soul.

—*SKS*, Bk. 2, p. 91

*F*ind such a place as mentioned above to be undisturbed. Sing *HU* aloud as *H-U*, one letter at a time. Let your body begin to rock in a gentle way that feels natural to you—side to side or back and forth—for as long as you wish.

Then become still with the Sound Current. Listen and perceive.

*   *   *

Look for the rhythms that run through your day—the flow of traffic, the ticking of a clock, the timing of meals. Let the Master show you how all life invisibly moves to the Sound Current.

Your Body of ECK

It is to be remembered that the life-giving part of the air inhaled is not chiefly the oxygen, which is absorbed into the bloodstream through the functioning of the lungs, but the ECK, which is essential to all the psychophysical activities of the body and mind, as well as the Soul, in the lower worlds.

—*SKS*, Bk. 2, p. 91

*B*reathing in, envision the ECK entering and nourishing your every cell and atom with Its divine power.

As you go through your day, take note of how your body is an instrument for the ECK. You may find yourself in just the right place to be of help to someone or take care of something for the greater good. It can be as small as picking up another's trash or holding the door for someone.

There is a greater meaning to these services. Act with love, and the Mahanta will take you behind the scenes.

Aids to Spiritual Living

> Therefore, all things which serve as obstacles in life must be considered as aids on the path of ECK. The underlying principle is that all trials and tribulations must be regarded as aids to spiritual living.
>
> —*SKS*, Bk. 2, p. 94

*O*pen *The Shariyat* to this passage, and read the parable that follows. Carefully note each detail of the story.

In contemplation, now see yourself in the role of the traveler walking in the night. Make this experience and realization your own. It will serve you well.

*   *   *

Life will present you with a perfect opportunity to use the inner wisdom this spiritual exercise can give you. It is both deeper and simpler than it may appear.

For the Joy of Selflessness

Transmutation into the true worlds of God is a spiritual process dependent upon the Spiritual Exercises of Eckankar. Its purpose is to aid the ECKist, both mentally and spiritually, to realize the complete selflessness of the ECKshar state of the heavenly worlds to which he has always aspired.

—*SKS*, Bk. 2, p. 95

*C*hant the word *ECKshar* for five to ten minutes or so. In your Spiritual Eye, see yourself standing on the shoreline of a great body of water, just before dawn. The Master comes for you in a small boat, and lets you take the oars. As you row away from the shores of the little self, watch the sun rise on the horizon. Give your all to this experience.

*   *   *

In your daily life, you can expect to experience selflessness in new ways. This brings a greater light to Soul.

To Resolve Conflict

> The word is *HU*, the universal name of God, which is in the language of every living thing. It is everywhere, in everything.
>
> —*SKS*, Bk. 2, p. 100

*I*f you find yourself in a stalemate of conflict with someone, take time to go into contemplation and sing *HU*. Inwardly invite the person of interest to join you in the love song to God.

Be willing to take responsibility for your part in the conflict. And give the entire matter to the Mahanta for the good of the whole.

The Confidence of Soul

Rebazar Tarzs once said, "Let your faith, your inner trust and confidence stream forth; remove your inner obstacles and open yourself to truth." It is this kind of faith, or inner awareness and open-mindedness, which finds its spontaneous expression, its liberation from an overwhelming psychic pressure, in the sacred sound of the HU. In this mantric sound all the positive and forward-pressing forces of the human, which are trying to blow up its limitations and burst the fetters of ignorance, are united and concentrated on the ECK, like an arrow point.

—*SKS*, Bk. 2, p. 101

*R*ead this passage aloud to yourself, slowly. Listen with your spiritual ears for the deep meaning in every sentence and phrase. Take your time with this.

Then go into contemplation, singing *HU*. The Master awaits your exploration of truth.

He will present ways to accept the freedom and confidence of Soul in your daily life and spiritual exercises. Be open-minded.

Beauty of Living

The ECK is the root and background of all life, all religions and daily living. It is the principle by which all life, the entire universes of God go forward. It is truth, and it is beauty.

—*SKS*, Bk. 2, pp. 101–2

*A*t day's end, briefly reflect on your experiences, both notable and mundane. Softly chant *chaitanya* (CHIE-tahn-yah), a word for the embodiment of all attributes of life, of vitality and vibrancy.

The Mahanta will show you an unseen treasure underlying the course of your day.

A New Start

It is the first and most important task of Eckankar to bend and restring the bow of Soul by proper training and discipline. After the self-confidence of man has been restored, the new doctrine of ECK has been firmly established, and the ornaments and cobwebs of theology and metaphysical speculation have withered and fallen before the sacred word of HU, it can again be attached to the Spiritual Exercises of ECK.

—*SKS*, Bk. 2, p. 102

Choose a sacred word, or use *HU* or your secret word, for this exercise.

In your Spiritual Eye, imagine meeting the Mahanta on a grassy hilltop while the sun is high. He holds a gleaming golden bow. A quiver of arrows is set against a nearby tree. As you sing your chosen word, a string manifests in the hand of the Master that vibrates with the sound of your word. The Master has come to restring the bow of Soul. You will find this a sacred moment.

The Master then asks you, "What do the arrows represent?" Continue your contemplation.

For True Hearing

What the Mahanta, the Living ECK Master teaches in words is only a fraction of what he teaches by his mere presence, his personality, and his living example. The Mahanta is always conscious of his own worldly shortcomings and limitations of words and speech, which cause him to hesitate to teach the works of ECK by putting into words something that is too profound and subtle to be grasped by mere logic and ordinary reasoning.

—*SKS*, Bk. 2, p. 104

*C*hoose a story from a book or talk by the Living ECK Master to read or listen to for this experience.

Sing Z for a minute or two, before listening or reading. Know that your inner ears are being opened to let truth enter your being. Visualize this.

The Master's love will heighten your awareness, and you will catch the subtle message for you.

An Experience of Soul

By the reversal of the viewpoint from the physical to the high level of Soul, all things suddenly appear in a new perspective insofar as the inner and outer world become equal and mutually dependent on the state of the higher consciousness. This consciousness, according to the degree of its development, experiences a different kind of reality, a different world, that of the Gakko, the world of being, in which all true ECK initiates dwell.

—*SKS*, Bk. 2, p. 105

*I*n a clean and quiet place, shut your eyes and see yourself meeting Wah Z in a Golden Wisdom Temple on the inner planes. Columns of translucent alabaster rise fifty feet high. There is a most beautiful, intriguing echo of your footsteps as you walk through the temple together.

You reach an alcove and seat yourself, and now there is a beautiful silence. Profound, expectant.

After a moment he instructs you to chant *Gakko* and enter the world of being.

CHAPTER 6

The Records of the Kros

A Visit to Katsupari

These records are history and prophecy. So in the beginning it is known that the records of the Kros are hidden in the Katsupari Monastery, under the guardianship of the great ECK Master Fubbi Quantz. This monastery is remotely found in the Buika Magna mountain range.

—*SKS*, Bk. 2, p. 107

*T*he Mahanta invites you to visit the Katsupari Monastery. Shut your eyes and begin by singing *Buika Magna*. A striking mountain range may appear in your inner vision. You may feel a sudden rush of wind as you approach a hidden entrance to the monastery. Now sing *HU*.

Fubbi Quantz welcomes all sincere students. He may ask you about this or that. Answer his questions carefully. This visit will be the first in a series of such meetings as you study this *Shariyat* chapter.

*   *   *

The knowledge you gain here offers a keener view of the world around you. You may find yourself less likely to take things at face value or to make snap judgments.

Watch for the wisdom this brings.

75

For Love of the Sound Current

Language, mind, and reality were uppermost in the thoughts of the people of this age. The idea, entirely unfamiliar to the modern world, that nature and language were inwardly akin was the mainstay of this age. The mantra of the HU was the sacred chant of all the people in the Satya Yuga.

—*SKS*, Bk. 2, p. 112

*T*ake a walk in nature with the Inner Master. Sing *HU* in conscious communication with the Life Force, the ECK. Listen to every sound as if it were speaking to you—the rustle of leaves, drone of a plane, song of a bird.

* * *

You will find you become more aware of how the holy Sound Current manifests in all forms, animate and inanimate. This realization can inspire you to take more care with people, pets, plants, and even things.

Atlantis Past and Present

Atlantis was first known about twenty-five to thirty thousand years ago. Its inhabitants were chiefly tall, white-skinned, fair-haired people with blue eyes who spoke a mixture of Lemurian and what was earlier considered a Scandinavian dialect. They were great sailors and traded abroad with the remnants of the old empire of Lemuria, around the areas of the China Sea and the Far East.

—*SKS*, Bk. 2, pp. 113–14

*I*n contemplation, sing the word *ECK-Vidya*. Ask the Mahanta to show you any past life you may have had in this era, and clues to its bearing on your life today.

Imagine he escorts you to a library on the inner planes and hands you a particular book. You accept the book and see there is an illustration on the cover. It may be a geometric symbol, a map, or the face of a person. There is also a word to note or chant. Follow the Inner Master's guidance.

*   *   *

This may bring a cleanup of something in your life. A relationship may polish itself, a knot may untangle, or a satisfying resolution to an old problem may unfold.

Be aware of this action of the Mahanta's love.

For True Perception

Maya itself, however, is not illusion in a manner of speaking, but the way that man looks at reality. The illusion is within himself. So he who masters this power gets the tool of liberation in his hand, the magic power of ECK: the power of creation, transformation, and reincarnation.

—*SKS*, Bk. 2, p. 116

*S*ing *HU* or your secret word. Imagine the Master gently touching your Spiritual Eye with his fingertip. You may feel a burst of Light and Sound enter your Tisra Til, or you may hear a specific inner sound—a ringing bell or chime. You may also feel an inner wind sweep through your being.

*   *   *

Practice true perception in your daily life. There will be something you are ready to overlook, but the Inner Master will in some way say, "Look again."

What happens next is key.

An Antidote to Fear

This is the way the divine Sugmad outwardly and inwardly moves toward the fullness of Its reality into inner awareness; and Soul is that part of man's being which has the power to ascend and descend the steps toward the heavenly worlds.

—*SKS*, Bk. 2, p. 116

*W*henever you feel fear, self-doubt, or stress of any kind, visualize the Master at the foot of an infinite staircase. He is inviting you to step up higher into the worlds of God's love for you.

*   *   *

When you accept the Master's invitation, you will be given a chance to make it easier for another Soul to take a step forward. Will you share the HU? Help someone clean up an error? Avoid giving criticism?

There is a gift for you in acting on your new awareness.

The Cosmic World Chain

He also becomes aware of his interrelationship with nations, races, civilizations, humanity, planets, solar systems, and finally the whole universe. He arrives at the perception of a cosmic world chain which begins with himself and ends in the Ocean of Love and Mercy of the Sugmad.

—*SKS*, Bk. 2, p. 117

*L*ook on pages 98–100 of *The Shariyat Ki Sugmad, Book Two*, for the sacred words of the inner planes. You can also find them on a Worlds of ECK chart. Softly sing the word for each plane three times, beginning with *Alayi* for the Physical Plane, and continuing through *HU* for the Anami Lok.

*   *   *

As you go through your day, try to be aware of your personal relationship with every event, each person you meet, everything you touch, each star you see in the sky. This can be perceived using your Spiritual Eye.

You will gain more awareness of your responsibility for your presence, wherever you are, whatever you do.

Tracing Your Past

> The emotion which surrounds a memory is part
> of the test about a past life. It is the most accurate
> of memories for anyone's past lives. This type of
> shadowy emotion can hang about for a long time
> on the threshold of consciousness before the im-
> ages clarify sufficiently to become tangible to the
> chela.
>
> —*SKS*, Bk. 2, p. 120

*H*ave you an inexplicable emotion tied to a place,
culture, historical period, geography, or even food? Take
this partial memory into contemplation. Using your
Spiritual Eye, picture this emotion as a shadow.

Shut your eyes and begin to sing *HU*. Use your inner
creativity, and the Master will help you turn the shadow
into light. Enjoy this transformation!

* * *

In your outer life, this light from your inner world
may illuminate clues to your history and the reason for
your emotion. Look for the connections.

For Unconditional Love

> The Sugmad supplies what is necessary for each Soul as well as for every other aspect of the person. The Sugmad knows whom It has called, and Its call is based on that knowledge of the individual, of his needs as well as his gifts.
>
> —*SKS*, Bk. 2, p. 124

*T*ake several relaxing breaths, and listen to the silence for a moment. Begin to chant *Sugmad* in whatever way seems right. Experiment with this as you go deeper into contemplation.

As you open the inner awareness to your Creator, feel yourself, as Soul, become one with Sugmad's unconditional love for you.

* * *

To let this awareness grow within you, find ways to give your unconditional love to others. There will be defined opportunities to pass along the blessing.

You will receive more than you give.

For Self-Direction

The moment that any chela of Eckankar real-izes this great truth—that all things in his world are a manifestation of the mental activity which goes on within him, and therefore a building and destroying of his karma; and that the conditions and circumstances of his life only reflect the state of consciousness with which he is fused—life changes for him.

—*SKS*, Bk. 2, pp. 125–26

*S*ing *HU* or your secret word for several minutes. Imagine your state of consciousness emanating only purity and Light, a golden ᛖ symbol at the core. The Mahanta has placed it there. Let it overtake your mind and heart with its brilliance.

*   *   *

During your day, should you feel you are drifting off your spiritual center, visualize the ᛖ symbol at the heart of every thought and deed.

This is another way of doing everything in the name of the ECK.

For Conscious Choice

> One must think of the worlds as containing an infinite number of states of consciousness from which they may be viewed. These states are like rooms or mansions in the house of God. . . . Each room contains the events and circumstances of life with infinite situations already worked out but not activated. They are activated as soon as Soul enters in and magnetizes them with action. Each represents certain emotional activities.
>
> —*SKS*, Bk. 2, p. 126

*W*hat would bring more harmony to your daily life? More balance, detachment, trust, or love? Sing *HU* and reflect on this with the Inner Master.

Using your Spiritual Eye, picture a room in the mansion of God that holds the state of consciousness you desire. What does this room contain? How does it feel to enter the room? The Mahanta will show you its secrets.

*   *   *

Look for opportunities in your life to take a specific action related to your goal. This is how desires come true.

For True Faith

To move to another state or room, consciousness as it is generally known, necessitates a change in faith and beliefs. All that one has ever desired is already present and only waits to be matched by his faith.

—*SKS*, Bk. 2, p. 127

sk the Mahanta for an experience in your inner or outer life that can only be proved by your faith. Do this with your whole heart and being.

The strength you gain will open a new door in your spiritual life.

CHAPTER 7

The Renunciation of Life

Answering the Call

The call of God to the individual to serve is not always for the same purpose in life, such as serving directly through work in a monastery or other sacred place, but often in the ways of a career or motherhood. Yet it is the means of perfecting that person called and is, therefore, the sphere within which he can be of most use to others.

—*SKS*, Bk. 2, p. 130

*B*egin your day by envisioning your home, work environment, or wherever you are as a sacred place where you are acting on the call of God to serve. Dedicate yourself accordingly. You are in holy service to life itself.

Your love for the Sugmad, the ECK, and the Mahanta will make it so.

A Life of Worship

There never was a time when man did not have the opportunity to accept ECK, for it has always been before him, although so many times he could never see his opportunity to grasp it. It has always been a life of worship, and the life of heaven can only be expressed in terms of sheer worship and adoration.

—*SKS*, Bk. 2, pp. 130–31

*S*incere gratitude is a form of worship.

As you go through your day, consciously look for at least three things you have never expressed gratitude for. Pause and give whatever it is, or whoever it is, your full attention and appreciation.

In so doing, you are accepting more of God's love.

Live as the Mahanta

At the heart of ECK life lies the conviction that the ECK is the way as well as the goal. Therefore, whether the way is long or short, and whatever blind corners it has, every moment is as important as the goal. It is only because to live as the Mahanta that to die is to gain.

—*SKS*, Bk. 2, p. 131

*O*pen the *Shariyat-Ki-Sugmad*, Book Two, to page 131, and read the last paragraph for more on the value of this very moment.

Softly sing *HU* or your secret word as you contemplate Soul's communication with God.

*　　*　　*

During your day, keep this love song to God humming in your being, just at the edge of your awareness. You will find you are more alert and better able to direct your thoughts and emotions.

Mastership Training

> The history of the world would be totally different without the influence of the ECK Masters and those who have followed ECK over the centuries, from the beginning of time in the physical universe. It was the ECK Masters who civilized the human race, who kept not only learning and even literacy alive, but taught the primitives farming and, during the latter ages after the golden era, the raising of cattle. Those who have done the most for the human race in its intellectual and spiritual aspects, as well as its materialistic life, have been the ECK Masters of the Ancient Order of the Vairagi.
>
> —*SKS*, Bk. 2, p. 133

*D*o you travel, use the Internet, get medical help, read, or listen to music? These are blessings of the Vairagi.

Sing *HU*, and open your heart in gratitude.

One or more of the ECK Masters may pay a visit to acknowledge your appreciation. Don't doubt it.

*   *   *

In your daily life, you can expect a chance to offer a gift of service to another.

It may come as a gentle nudge, as a suggestion from someone in your day, or through a dream. It will be part of your own training for Mastership.

92

The Golden Ladder

The life in Eckankar is made for the active Souls and is purely an individual search for God. It is not a battle with the Kal, which those who believe in the worldly affairs are confronted with daily. As long as the individual looks at his daily battles with the Kal, his attention will always be upon this and not upon the ECK. He must constantly look to the ECK for his salvation, his way to freedom, and never to any limitations.

—*SKS*, Bk. 2, p. 134

*I*n contemplation, sing *Wah Z* and imagine he is helping you climb a golden ladder of ECK. Each rung symbolizes either a blessing or a challenge in your life. When you get to the rungs of challenge, he whispers a word or phrase into your ear. It will keep your attention aligned with the ECK.

Remember this during your day.

To Reach for Truth

No person can have the goodness of God in his life unless he is obedient to the spiritual laws; and often, when asked, he could not even give one. Therefore, it appears that man has forgotten his own image in God.

—*SKS*, Bk. 2, pp. 135–36

*O*pen *The Spiritual Laws of Life*, and look for a law you may be unfamiliar with. Read a passage or two about it.

Take this into contemplation, and let the Mahanta show you how practicing this principle can remind you of your true nature and identity. There is another benefit to this exercise.

You will be given more than one chance to apply your understanding and extend your reach for truth.

It will be worth the effort.

Lessons on Love

Soul is free to do whatever It desires as long as it falls within a general pattern of the heavenly law. This law is: Love is all, and do as thou wilt.

This means that all Souls who enter into the heavenly state must abide by the law which they establish for themselves. The self-abiding law is for the individual Soul to recognize that It is Its own law. First of all, It must love or give out goodwill to all beings within the heavenly worlds. Secondly, It must make Its own law to abide by, and this must be in harmony with the great law: Love all things.

—SKS, Bk. 2, p. 138

*O*pen your heart to the Mahanta, and ask him to show you this higher law of love in action. To prepare, read chapter 20, "Purity," in *Stranger by the River,* by Paul Twitchell. Your experience may be one of action, observation, or insight.

Before going to bed, take some time to lightly contemplate the events of your day. Soul will recognize the Master's lesson.

For the Viewpoint of Love

When Soul enters into the regions of immortality, the worlds of true Spirit above the psychic worlds, It finds no opposites. Light is light and there is no opposite to it and the sounds of ECK, only the polarity of the highest qualities.

—*SKS*, Bk. 2, p. 138

*S*oftly sing the word *Lamakan,* a word for the endless, the beyond all, the eternal.

Meet the Mahanta as he walks toward you from the center of an enormous, brilliant sun. Hear the sound of its brilliance, and of the love of the Master.

Soul has heard this before.

The Lives of Spiritual Giants

> One reaps great spiritual benefits by placing himself where the gains are to be made. Thus, if he reads the lives of the spiritual giants and lives quietly in a place where the life of ECK is greater, he gains in his unfoldment. However, he does not gain unless he practices the Spiritual Exercises of ECK regularly.
>
> —*SKS*, Bk. 2, p. 140

*F*ind a quiet place where you will not be interrupted. Begin this exercise by recalling all the names of the ECK Masters you have heard of. One by one, picture their faces if you can, or some other aspect of their appearance. More will come to you. It's in the doing.

You may be surprised at what you recall on the inner planes.

*   *   *

Choose an ECK Adept to research. You can look in *Those Wonderful ECK Masters* and other ECK books to further your research on the inner and outer. This study will develop your spiritual stamina.

Purification and Protection

To react or to respond to anything is to be in sympathy with it and therefore become a part of it, itself. There is the law of Kal that if anyone responds to worry, he establishes fresh cause for worry. All men have a tendency to let themselves become slaves to the Kal power.

—*SKS*, Bk. 2, p. 141

*S*ing *HU* or your secret word, and bathe yourself in a waterfall of Light and Sound. See it cleansing all your bodies with purity and spiritual vitality. Enjoy this purification and healing.

Now watch as the Master offers you a shield to wear as protection—a buffer between you and events of your day. It could appear as a vibratory field of neutrality, a warm glowing light, or a polished mirror.

*   *   *

Self-discipline activates this protection. You will gain the viewpoint of Soul.

The Organic Whole

The sense of the wholeness of things is perhaps the most typical feature of the ECKist mind. The mind of man in the psychic worlds divides, specializes, and thinks in terms of categories; the ECKist instinct is the opposite, to take the widest view, to see things as an organic whole. This is the strength of the ECKist who is able to face every problem in life and bring about his own solution to it without having to depend on another.

—*SKS*, Bk. 2, p. 147

*A*re you facing a problem within yourself? Close your eyes and sing *HU* sweetly with a pure heart. Picture your problem on the face of a coin. It can be a static image, a moving picture, or a word.

Pay attention as the Master takes the coin into his hand and turns it over. He will ask, "What do you see?" Continue to sing *HU* as you contemplate your answer.

To Listen and Love

> Those who love the Living ECK Master and are willing to give all their love to him will win everything in life. It is as though when one gives up life, he shall gain life.
>
> —*SKS*, Bk. 2, p. 148

*T*ake several deep, relaxing breaths. Begin by singing Z, and imagine you are meeting the Master by the shore of an ancient river. He invites you to talk about anything at all of interest or concern to you.

He is listening to your heart.

Are you?

You may have a sudden understanding of the true relationship between Soul and the Master. Accept whatever blessing is given.

*   *   *

Listening to others is a way to listen to the Mahanta. Look for these divine opportunities to give and receive the Master's love.

CHAPTER 8

ECK, the Sacred Teachings

Forming the Universe

Man cannot behold this universe as he could some spectacle before his own eyes for he, himself, is a part of it. He aids in its formation; he is, as it were, a fellow actor in a kind of drama, the variation of which depends upon his subjective life which expresses its manifold incidents.

—*SKS*, Bk. 2, p. 149

*T*oday, consecrate yourself as a clear vehicle to serve the good of the whole. See yourself as a transparency for the love and action of ECK.

Later, silently sing *HU* and look back over your day in the company of the Mahanta. What part did you play in the formation of the universe?

Maybe someone observed your actions, demeanor, or words. Or simply benefitted from seeing the light in your eyes.

Let the Master show you.

Breathing ECK

He must think of ECK as life. It is that essence, that fluid, or Holy Spirit which flows out of God to be used as the creative force for the feeding and maintenance of all things in every universe of the Sugmad, whether it be a piece of mineral, a particle of soil, an animal, or a man.

All the same, It is the basic reality, the chain of invisible atoms that man breathes for survival in the flesh, that he uses to create thought.

—*SKS*, Bk. 2, p. 152

Find a place that is quiet and calm. Begin by singing *E*...*C*...*K* aloud or inside yourself, one letter at a time for a few moments.

Feel your Spiritual Eye open wide to let in a greater vision of truth. See the very atoms of your breath as a gift from God.

*   *   *

As you move through your day, take time to respect all that is around you as a manifestation of God's love for Soul. Take special care of something within your environment to express your gratitude.

It will be a two-way love.

The Holy Fire

The inner illumination is the holy fire and is united with an infinite love for the divine reality. This inner flame, this simultaneous love and knowledge, when born, rises and grows until finally, through an impersonal ecstasy, the whole being of man is kindled with a supreme desire for the Sugmad.

—*SKS*, Bk. 2, pp. 154–55

*O*pen your heart and sing *SUGMAD* softly as a whisper. Look for the flame of Soul's love for God glowing with an infinite brilliance. It will warm you with its living light.

* * *

Be aware of how the Inner Master guides you to reach out to someone or something which could use your help this day. Act, and it will grow the holy fire within you.

True Riches

Man cannot hope to possess true riches greater than those he already bears within himself. He should use them and not neglect them, but they are so familiar that at times they do not appear to be of any value to him. Therefore, he pursues tawdry chattels whose possession is denied him, because man is so weak that the world is sometimes obliged to rebuff him to cause him to detach himself from the world.

—*SKS*, Bk. 2, p. 155

*D*uring this day, let the HU play in the background of your mind and thoughts.

Be grateful for occasions to use your divine creativity. Give some stubborn obstacle one more go at resolution. You may find a way around the problem or see possibilities not apparent to others.

Appreciate this chance to be in conscious communication with the ECK.

To See the Gift

> The Mahanta knows what things every individual who is under his protection has need of, before he asks of him.
>
> —*SKS*, Bk. 2, p. 156

*W*hen you face a challenge, immediately ask the Mahanta to help you see what you need from the situation. Open your heart to him and ask in purity—even gratitude.

Instantly, or in time, you will see how life is serving the unfoldment of Soul.

Living the Lesson

The wise man is he who realizes the transitory and illusory nature of the affairs of this world and makes the best use of his body and mind in service to the Sugmad. He thus derives benefit from all that the Sugmad, through Its grace, has placed in the body. He then takes that priceless jewel, the essence of all, the Atma, or Soul, to Its real abode.

—SKS, Bk. 2, p. 156

You are invited to join a Satsang class on the inner planes. They are discussing *vairag*, detachment. In contemplation, see yourself approaching a white gazebo set on a grassy hill, where the class is meeting. The pillars of the gazebo are resonant and act as amplifiers.

As you take a seat, an ECK Master leads a chant of the word *vairag*. Join in. You can expect to gain an insight about the relationship between detachment and divine love.

*   *   *

Don't worry if you do not recall the insight you received. Your day will give you a chance to live the lesson.

Living in the Heart

Free from thought, reality abides in the heart, the source of all thought. It is, therefore, called the heart by orthodox religionists and thinkers. To contemplate upon It one thinks of It as living in the heart of all things.

—*SKS*, Bk. 2, pp. 157-58

*S*ing *HU* with joy—like a child greeting a new day with wonder. In your contemplation, dedicate your heart and being as a pure channel for the love of the Sugmad, the ECK, and the Mahanta.

The Inner Master can now show you how the love of the Sugmad, the ECK, and the Mahanta lives in the heart of all things.

Light of the Sugmad

The Light of the Sugmad spreads into Soul, and thus descends into the various bodies—the Physical, Astral, Causal, and Mental, which It wants to use as a clear channel for Its own Light and Sound.

—*SKS*, Bk. 2, p. 160

*U*sing your Spiritual Eye, imagine you are standing with the Master on the shore of an ocean of light. The tide is coming in. Waves of light reach higher and higher—swirling, immersing, illuminating every atom of your being. The Master offers you his hand.

* * *

In some way, you will experience being a clear channel for the Light and Sound of God in your day. It will be a blessed occasion.

Regaining Ground

By the power of contemplation and the upward journey, the force of desire is lessened. Temporary suppression might lead one to think that it has been annihilated. But as long as Soul does not reach the Sat Lok region, desire cannot be fully eradicated. . . . One may falter, though soon recover strength and regain lost ground by the practice of the Spiritual Exercises of ECK and the help of the Mahanta, the Living ECK Master.

—*SKS*, Bk. 2, pp. 160–61

*L*ook for reminders from the Master to practice self-discipline today. They may be subtle and appear as common as your own passing thoughts.

Make it a waking spiritual exercise to act on three chances to strengthen yourself spiritually by acting on those reminders.

There will be inner rewards.

Akaha

The first and foremost region which is the highest and largest, the name and location of which cannot be described in mortal language, is that of the Sugmad, or Akaha, the end of all worlds, the Ocean of Love and Mercy. This is the beginning and the end of all; it circumscribes all worlds. It is the love and power of this world which is vibrating in every place, by the force of its first principle. . . . Only the ECK Masters and their followers ever have the opportunity to reach this plane.

—*SKS*, Bk. 2, p. 161

*R*ead this passage aloud to yourself. Hear every word. Then sing the word *Akaha* (ah-KAH-hah) for several minutes.

The Mahanta will begin to awaken you to the vibration of Akaha wherever you are, wherever you look, whenever you remember.

* * *

As you practice this, you will begin to see more of what each part of life has in common with the love of God. It can bring more peace, confidence, and calm to your days.

Beyond Appearance

> The primal Word, the Adi-ECK, manifests and moves into the lower worlds. It is that which gives the life substance to all things. It is not subject to destruction and change; It is always the same.
>
> —*SKS*, Bk. 2, p. 162

*C*hoose a place where you will be alone and at peace. Begin to chant *Adi-ECK* aloud. This is the primal God Force.

Experiment with the sound—try it different ways. Chant the word several times on the same breath, fast or slow. Use a whisper or a melody. Listen for the way that activates you inwardly.

*   *   *

This practice will give you an experience of spiritual sight. You will begin to see a situation or event from the viewpoint of the changeless state—beyond appearances.

You will be aware of this when it occurs.

113

Special Training

When Souls descend from the Ocean of Love and Mercy, they stay in the Soul Plane before entering into the psychic worlds. Each is given special training before entering the lower planes so that It can have a greater opportunity to escape the snares and traps of the Kal Niranjan, who will certainly try to keep It within the lower worlds as long as possible.

—*SKS*, Bk. 2, p. 162

*B*efore bed, sing *HU* with joy and gratitude for the freedom to grow in love and wisdom. Ask to receive a special training in the dream state to help you in your day tomorrow.

In the morning, make a few notes from dreams you recall. As you meet the day, you may find you are prepared to tackle an unexpected turn of events, or to take a new approach to some issue.

This may require a change of heart, of attitude, or of opinion. What will you do?

The Light of Truth

The Mahanta, the Living ECK Master has existed in this world for millions of years, and the works of ECK have been given to the selected chelas for millions of years. . . . The ECK Masters held up the spiritual truths as a torch lighting the way for all those who had eyes to see.

—*SKS*, Bk. 2, p. 165

*I*n contemplation, chant *Mahanta* as may-HON-tay for several minutes. Visualize a golden light streaming through a small window set in a heavy wooden door. The Mahanta will give you inspiration on how to open the door and receive more of the Light of God. Follow your guidance.

*   *   *

Expect to see the truth of something in your inner or outer world that was not evident to you before. It will be a welcome discovery.

115

CHAPTER 9

❧

The Visions of Lai Tsi

A Visit with Gopal Das

"Gopal Das is now the guardian of the fourth book of the Shariyat-Ki-Sugmad on the Astral Plane, while his two chelas are now ranked high in the Ancient Order of the Vairagi Adepts. Yaubl Sacabi is now the guardian of the second book of the Shariyat-Ki-Sugmad and the head of the spiritual city of Agam Des. Tomo Geshig is in the sixth world, the Alakh Lok, where he has charge of the Shariyat-Ki-Sugmad there."

—*SKS*, Bk. 2, p. 172

*C*hant the word *Kala* (kah-LAH) aloud for several minutes. This is the word for the Astral Plane.

The ECK Master Gopal Das invites you to the Temple of Askleposis. He may escort you to a library, a reception hall, or a quiet alcove in a busy mezzanine. His company is airy, sweet, and melodious.

At some point he will turn his gaze upon you. You will have found what you came for.

Lai Tsi's Prayer

"Here is a short contemplation seed which I found in myself upon returning from the heavenly worlds:

"'Show me Thy ways, O Sugmad;
Teach me Thy path.
Lead me in Thy truth, and teach me;
On Thee do I wait all day.
Remember, O Beloved, Thy guiding light
And Thy loving care.
For it has been ever Thy will,
To lead the least of Thy servants to Thee!'

"Should anyone be in distress or need to reach the great Sugmad, use this contemplation; repeat it slowly and it certainly brings results."

—*SKS*, Bk. 2, pp. 172–73

*K*now you are speaking directly to your Creator as you repeat these holy words.

Then you will want to listen.

Healing of Afflictions

"All those who gaze upon the countenance of the Mahanta, the Living ECK Master shall be lifted up spiritually and be healed of all their afflictions. This is the right act which strikes a cord that extends throughout the whole universe, touches all spiritual intelligence, visits every world, vibrates along its whole extent, and conveys its vibrations to the very bosom of the Sugmad."

—*SKS*, Bk. 2, p. 173

*D*o you look to replace fear with certainty? Anger with acceptance? Doubt with gratitude?

Choose an image of the Master, and look into his eyes. Still your mind, open your heart. Healing is his gift to you.

*   *   *

Watch for the opportunity to choose a course of action or approach to something that may seem to be out of character for you. If it looks to be the right thing to do, then do it.

This sends a signal into your world that you are ready for change.

121

Speaking with Truth

"To the enlightened man whose consciousness embraces the universe—to him the universe becomes his body, while his physical body becomes the manifestation of the ECK, his inner vision an expression of the higher truth, the highest reality, and his speech an expression of eternal truth."

—*SKS*, Bk. 2, p. 174

*C*hant the word *Dhunatmik* for as long as you care to in contemplation. It means the Voice of the Sugmad, the Sound that can't be spoken. Then listen for the echo within you.

*　　*　　*

Take special care in all you say today. Remind yourself it is a manifestation of the Sound Current.

Your day will be a journey of truth.

Neither For nor Against

"The secrets of ECK, the constant, formative way from which no event is exempt, is disclosed only to those who can be rid of their personal wishes or prejudices about the ECK. One comes to grips with It, as It lies hidden beneath appearances, by disregarding his own point of view. Prejudiced ears have no place on the path of ECK."

—*SKS*, Bk. 2, p. 175

*C*lose your eyes and sing the word *vairag*, the ECK word for detachment, for a few minutes. Welcome the ECK Current as you would a fresh, cool breeze on a hot and stuffy day. Watch It purify and refresh all within your heart and mind with Its blessings.

* * *

For one day, practice being neither for nor against. Good reminders to do this will come. Take a breath, sing *HU*, and let the ECK recharge your state of mind.

The Window of Heaven

"But man seeks too much the gold and silver of the world when he should be seeking the Window of Heaven through which, when opened, all the treasures that he believed were possible will now come pouring to him.

". . . None will know this until each has a glimpse of the broad skies and the beautiful gardens, the running waters and the wonderful colors of the world beyond, by the opening of the window."

—*SKS*, Bk. 2, p. 176

In contemplation, see yourself before the Window of Heaven, your Spiritual Eye. Yes, this can be done.

You are getting ready to open it. Are there draperies that need to be opened? Blinds or shutters? Is there a lock or security bar? Remove all the obstacles, one by one. The Mahanta is there to help.

You cannot see through the window until it is open. When the moment is right, the Master will show you how to release the latch. Do this, and open the window.

Your heart will receive the view with wonder.

For Liberty

"The passions of the worldly life are like heavy clouds which shut out the wisdom, like they shut out the sun entirely or obscure the brilliancy of its light. They may be compared to a violent wind which agitates the surface of the water so that it cannot reflect the splendor of the skies above, to the cocoon of the butterfly which deprives it of liberty, and to the shell of certain fruits which prevents their fragrance from diffusing itself abroad."

—*SKS*, Bk. 2, p. 178

*U*se this spiritual exercise when you feel discomfort due to being out of balance or caught up in the mind passions.

Begin by singing *HU* softly to yourself. Imagine that you are in a room with a very tall ceiling and pearl-white walls. There is a glowing gold ⚿ symbol in the middle of a wall. It has the power to remind you of your higher will.

Give it all your loving attention as you sing the holy name of God.

You will enjoy this sanctuary from the mind.

*   *   *

Welcome the subtle tests that will exercise your higher will. This can bring healing for even the most stubborn habits.

Firm as a Diamond

"The true Master of Eckankar is he who is familiar with the practice of daily virtues; who, with the sword of wisdom, has lopped off all the branches and cut through all the roots of the tree of evil and, with the light of reason, has dispelled the thick darkness by which he is enveloped; who, though surrounded by mountains of passion, meets all their assaults with a heart as firm as a diamond."

—*SKS*, Bk. 2, p. 180

*C*hoose a place of calm and quiet. Begin by chanting *Mahanta*, first aloud, then silently.

Using your Spiritual Eye, see your heart as a living diamond of Light and Sound. You may see brilliant colors, feel a purifying surge, or hear the sound of light alive with ECK. This is the radiant love of the Master.

Go through your day knowing you will learn and profit from whatever comes your way.

The Seed of Understanding

"All that has been, all that is, everything that will be, everything that ever has been said—are to be found in the Shariyat-Ki-Sugmad. But the works within these sacred books do not explain themselves, and they can only be understood when the Mahanta, the Living ECK Master has removed the garments with which they are clothed and scattered the clouds that veil their celestial light."

—*SKS*, Bk. 2, p. 181

*W*hen you want a deeper understanding of some passage you read in this chapter of *The Shariyat*, go into light contemplation.

Chant *Wah Z*, and imagine the Master reading the passage in question aloud to you. When he's done, he gently touches your Spiritual Eye. Come out of contemplation when you are ready, and read the passage again.

Contemplate the words knowing you have the seed of understanding within you.

Seals of the Mind

"The words are seals of the mind—results or, more correctly, stations—of an infinite series of experiences which reach from an unimaginably distant past into the present, and which feel their way into an equally unimaginably distant future. They are the audible that clings to the inaudible, the forms and potentialities of Soul, that which grows and unfolds into perfection."

—*SKS*, Bk. 2, p. 182

Choose a word from *The Shariyat* or from *A Cosmic Sea of Words: The ECKANKAR Lexicon* that carries special meaning for you.

Experiment with ways to use this word in contemplation. You may simply look at the word inwardly or outwardly, write it thirty times or more, or sing it syllable by syllable or letter by letter.

Put your heart into it. There is a special reason you chose this word.

The Inner Master is ready to show you.

The Greater Form

"The seer, the poet and singer, the spiritually creative, the psychically receptive and sensitive, and the saint—all know about the essentiality of form in word and sound, in the visible and the tangible. They do not dislike what appears small or insignificant, because they can see the great in the small. Through them the Word becomes flesh, and the sounds and signs of which It is formed become the vehicle of mysterious forces."

—*SKS*, Bk. 2, p. 183

*D*uring your day, the Master will draw your attention to some small event or detail. It may be anything at all, but it will be special in some way. Note this to reflect on later.

Before bed, revisit this in your mind as you sing *HU* or your secret word. Imagine you are viewing it through a special ECK telescope that reveals its greater significance for you. It may be the seed of a spiritual lesson, a reminder of a dream, or a clue to a past life important to you today.

This practice will train your inner awareness.

Expanding Truth

"The ECK has existed throughout all eternity, yet from ancient times until now, from the beginning, the ECK has been presented under an endless number of names. How may I know you know It? By what can you tell It? It is known only through your insights, your intuitions, your experiences with what is eternal, and what you know as truth."

—*SKS*, Bk. 2, p. 185

*W*hat do you know as truth?

Shut your eyes, and sing *HU* for several minutes. As answers come to you, watch for the one that seems to come alive when you think of it. It may appear as a feeling, a thought, a memory, or an experience.

*　　*　　*

The Mahanta will bring you an experience in your inner or outer life to expand your certainty of truth.

A priceless gift.

Rewards of Yielding

"He who can yield, can survive both here in life and in the invisible worlds. This is what makes marriages last throughout the years, what makes friendships everlasting, what makes nations friendly in relation to one another, and what allows Soul to live in eternity."

—*SKS*, Bk. 2, p. 187

*D*o you find it difficult to yield?

In this spiritual exercise, take long, slow, deep breaths, and imagine you are breathing in the HU. It reaches into your lungs and heart. Spend several minutes aligning yourself with God's love in this way.

In your daily life, the Mahanta will bring you an exercise in yielding. Remember to sing *HU* as you consider your options.

You may find this an enjoyable, rewarding experience as you gain more self-control and become a greater channel for the ECK.

CHAPTER 10

&

The Arch of
the Heavenly World

The Soul of All Beings

"The Mahanta is he who exists by himself and who is in all because all is in him. It is he who exists by himself, because Soul alone can perceive him who cannot be apprehended by the physical senses. It is he who is without visible parts, except the human body, but is eternal—the Soul of all beings— none can comprehend him except those who live in the high worlds of ECK in the Atma Sarup."

—*SKS*, Bk. 2, p. 191

*C*hant *Mahanta* as may-HON-tay for five minutes or so. See yourself meeting with the Master somewhere familiar to you—your office, kitchen, or ECK center.

His smile warms you—you are old and dear friends. At a certain moment he will whisper, "I am always with you" into your ear.

It may feel like a wind blowing through you or a soft light bathing your heart. It may take you beyond your body to the secret worlds of your being.

At any time of the day or night, you can hear this when you need to.

Hear it now.

Your Gifts

Truth, goodness, love, and beauty are commonly regarded as poetic ideas, but they are, in essence, spiritual facts. These are the ideas which one should include in his speech and thoughts. They are the language of Soul and must bring about an awakening of that pervading, persuasive urge in man to realize himself in his totality, as a being essentially spiritual and eternal. Truth as given by the ECK is neither esoteric, strange, nor fanciful. It is at once sublime, universal, and profoundly practical.

—*SKS*, Bk. 2, p. 193

*R*ead this passage aloud to yourself.

Today the Master will guide you to give gifts of truth, goodness, love, or beauty to others.

In contemplation, sing *seva* (see-VAH) for several minutes. It is a spiritual word that means a service of love, and it will open your heart to the giving nature of Soul.

*   *   *

Reflect on this exercise at the end of your day. Begin by singing *seva* again, and follow the Mahanta's footprints as you retrace your day.

136

Your Higher Nature

If truth is to be of actual value, it must be experienced and manifested in the chela's life. The ECKist is the truly spiritual man, is the most giving of all men. His universal vision naturally compels him to see the presence of the Mahanta in all beings, and he unceasingly speaks to the essential nature of all beings. His very existence inspires others to manifest their own higher nature.

—*SKS*, Bk. 2, p. 193

In your contemplation, chant your secret word or *HU.* Open your heart to the Mahanta as he prepares you to be an inspiration to others.

He may take you to a Temple of Golden Wisdom where the Light of ECK runs like a living river through the corridors. It will be quite remarkable. Step into this moving stream, and your experience will continue.

* * *

In your day, pay attention to your interactions with others, and remember the Mahanta's preparation. There will be reminders.

Peace and Selflessness

The mystery of peace is found only within one, and he has to distribute his state of selflessness to others to bring degrees of peace; that is, if they are ready and willing to accept this quality of God within themselves. Each environment is unique within itself and must be treated differently by the chela who is desirous of bringing peace within its boundaries.

—*SKS*, Bk. 2, p. 194

*S*ing the word *Shanti* for several minutes. Let the peace of ECK shine in your heart.

Sing this word silently to yourself when you are in tense or troubling situations—not to change the situation, but to bring calm upliftment to your own being.

See yourself as the eye of the storm—a neutral beacon of ECK's blessings.

Then, follow your heart.

The Unbreakable Thread

ECK is the thread—so fine as to be invisible, yet so strong as to be unbreakable—which binds together all beings in all the worlds of God, in all universes, throughout all time, and beyond time into eternity.

—*SKS*, Bk. 2, p. 196

In a clean, quiet place, begin by chanting the word *aditi* (ah-DEE-tee), another word for eternity.

Using your Spiritual Eye, see the golden thread of ECK connecting you, your family, your friends, your community, your nation, and all of life. This includes the Mahanta, every ECK Master in the Vairagi Order, and the Nine Silent Ones.

*   *   *

When you find yourself focusing on the limitations of others, stop. Take a moment to switch gears and, instead, recognize the highest potential of ECK in every Soul, including yourself.

139

Akshar Discipline

Each new spiritual experience, as well as each new situation in life, widens the perception of each chela and brings about a subtle transformation within all concerned. Thus the spiritual nature of the disciples of the Mahanta changes continually, not only the conditions of life, because it is the law of all life to either progress or degenerate. If there is strict obedience to the will of the ECK, there shall be no problem for any initiate who is desirous of reaching the Akshar, the imperishable consciousness.

—*SKS*, Bk. 2, pp. 197–98

Shut your eyes, take three deep breaths, and chant the word *Akshar* for five minutes or so. Visualize yourself carried on the winds of ECK toward your highest spiritual goals for this lifetime.

Open your wings to your future.

* * *

Today, in a particular situation, you will be presented with a choice, a chance to go forward in spiritual understanding. If you miss it, it will come to you a second time. And a third.

Check your inner compass often.

The Proper Time

Discrimination is, therefore, practiced by the Mahanta, the Living ECK Master in order to be an example for those who follow him. He tries to show each individual, personally, what is best for him. The enlightenment is never forced upon those who do not care for it or who are not ripe for it. It is given only to those who thirst for higher knowledge, and it is given at the proper time and the proper place.

—*SKS*, Bk. 2, p. 200

*S*ing *HU* for a time as you reflect on your thirst for truth in this lifetime.

On the inner planes of your being, the Mahanta escorts you to the fountain of enlightenment. He has brought a cup for you to drink from.

It is filled with his love for you.

What does your cup tell you about your thirst for truth?

Golden Acts

Spiritual unfoldment can be found in the little things of life. The drama and fixed things which are getting the attention of man are generally those of the Kal. It is the nature of the Kal to force man's attention to the dramatic things of life, such as war and politics. But it is in the small events, such as goodness in the daily things of life, being kind to a child, speaking softly to those who can be hurt easily, noninjury to a fellow creature, and the giving of one's self to others who are without the essentials of life, that spiritual unfoldment can be found.

—*SKS*, Bk. 2, pp. 200–201

This day is an opportunity to be a fully conscious channel for the Mahanta in some natural way right for you.

In contemplation, sing *HU* with all your goodness. The Mahanta brings you a beautiful notebook and a golden pen. He invites you to record your golden acts of kindness at the end of the day.

Just one act can fill the whole book with its impact.

Reshape History

If the individual man will keep up the Spiritual
Exercises of ECK, it's found that this process of
spiritual growth is repeated and experienced in him.
It does not only mean that the individual will become the connecting link between the past, the
present, and the future, but that his past will become
revitalized and the present rejuvenated in his experiences. It also transforms itself into the creative
process of the future. In this way history is reshaped
for the individual into his present life and becomes
a part of his own being.

—*SKS*, Bk. 2, p. 201

*O*pen *The Shariyat*, and read the rest of the paragraph quoted above.

Begin by chanting *ECK-Vidya* six times. Envision the
myriad events of your life plotted on a time line stretching out before you. Now watch as the ECK sweeps along
the graph, like a wind swirling autumn leaves.

You may hear or feel the winds of ECK transforming
these events and memories into a pattern of Light and
Sound.

*   *   *

In daily life you may find that you are free of a
troubling memory, or that you understand the purpose
of a difficult situation from the past.

For Victory

No sacrifice that one makes for another is in vain, even if it is not recognized or is misused by those for whose benefit it was intended. Each sacrifice is an act of renunciation, a victory over ourselves, and an act of liberation.

—*SKS*, Bk. 2, p. 202

*C*ompletely open yourself to the ECK as you sing *HU*.

See the door of your heart open to let the waves of the Ocean of Love and Mercy enter without limitation. Feel them washing away any limitations such as self-interest, greed, pride, or vanity. Relish this rejuvenation.

Life will quickly offer you the chance to manifest this new state of being.

A Devotee of the Sugmad

The Sugmad says It lives neither in heaven above nor on earth below, nor in any paradise, but It lives in the hearts of Its devotees who love It.

—*SKS*, Bk. 2, p. 204

*B*egin by chanting *Sugmad* for ten minutes or so. Chant from your heart center, and let the vibration fill your being, spilling out into the world.

*   *   *

Imagine your heart as a home for the Sugmad all day. With your love, it will be so.

Secrets of Spiritual Practices

Some believe that the scriptures are the highest one can receive from the Mahanta, the Living ECK Master. But this is not true. The secrets of spiritual practices, which can be known only by the Mahanta, cannot be reduced to writing, nor are they clearly mentioned in any scriptures. There are only vague references to them here and there. They serve only as a testimony in those writings. The complete secret can only be imparted by the Mahanta.

—*SKS*, Bk. 2, p. 204

*O*n the inner planes, meet with the Mahanta somewhere you have never visited in a spiritual exercise before—perhaps a waterfall, a bonfire at the ocean, or a ledge on the side of a cliff.

Give some thought to your choice.

Sit with the Master, and begin by just listening to the sounds in your environment. At a certain point, he will invite you to close your eyes and go into contemplation. Now you will receive instruction for a spiritual practice to try.

You will want to keep this to yourself.

CHAPTER 11

&

The Culture of Eckankar

A Noticeable Difference

Those who follow the teachings of the Mahanta, the Living ECK Master generally form an inner community which is noticeable on those planes beyond this world. . . . It can be said that the ECK society is that which is within the whole of the mainstream of any society, in any nation, or on any plane beyond this realm.

—*SKS*, Bk. 2, p. 209

*A*s you go about your day, be aware of yourself as part of the ECK society. Look for the difference this awareness can make in your approach and dealings with others. The Mahanta will give you reminders.

You may be more tolerant, respectful, content, or confident. You are a living part of the ECK culture wherever you are, whatever you do.

Seeking What Is True

This is called a culture within a culture, for the ECK, working as a force, uses Its own, individually or collectively, to bring about changes in various environments. Outwardly, a true follower of ECK is not concerned with reform. He is seeking what is true, and that very search has transforming effects on society.

—*SKS*, Bk. 2, p. 209

*O*pen your Spiritual Eye by singing *HU* or your secret word for a few moments. Declare yourself a pure vehicle for the unconditional love of God.

Observe the Light and Sound of ECK as It imbues the pattern of your thoughts and deeds and the actions of your heart.

*   *   *

By seeking truth in this way, you can find wisdom, freedom, and unfoldment in any place at any time.

Ready to Serve

Those who have reached the Fifth Initiation, that which is called the Mahdis, are banded together in deep spiritual ties, which act as one for all, and all for one. . . . They are few in number, but once anyone becomes a member of this precious little band, he never turns back—he never leaves it and his goal is always forward, to give help to the rest of the world. He must always be ready to serve those less fortunate than himself.

—*SKS*, Bk. 2, pp. 210–11

*I*n your contemplation, chant the word *Moksha* for several minutes. This is a word for freedom from rebirth—a part of the Fifth Initiation. You may have the sensation of coming out of a cocoon, a shell, or a shadow. The Master will show the next step.

*   *   *

Today there will be a distinct opportunity to give of yourself for another. It may be as simple as listening, having patience, or offering a helping hand to a neighbor.

Regardless of your initiation level, it will take you one step closer to God.

The Secret Entrance

Only those who have entered into the ECK and have gained the higher degrees of enlightenment through the Mahanta, the Living ECK Master have been able to enter into the community of heaven. The secret of entrance into this holy community is through submission to the Mahanta, the Living ECK Master. To give up, to surrender oneself to him, will bring about an opening of the door to the heavenly worlds where dwell those who are the beloved of the Mahanta, the Living ECK Master.

—*SKS*, Bk. 2, pp. 211–12

*S*ing *Mahanta* as a simple melody from your heart. Visualize meeting the Master on the inner planes where he leads you to a spacious gallery of illuminated doorways.

He will open one particular door and invite you to enter a world of new beginnings.

* * *

Of special note: There will be something in your life that you need to give or give up to complete this experience.

A Visit to Honardi

Instead of joining such orders, they should seek the perfect Master, the Mahanta, the Living ECK Master and spend their time in his service. They would be taught to perform the inner spiritual exercises and would become ascetics in the true sense of the word. Instead of wasting their time, they would eventually reach their true home, the spiritual community of Honardi, in the world of the Atma Lok, the fifth region of Soul.

—*SKS*, Bk. 2, p. 213

In contemplation, sing the word *Honardi* slowly for several minutes. This spiritual community welcomes visitors who come to attune themselves to its purpose. The Mahanta will escort you there. Using your Spiritual Eye, look for a pale golden light, and listen for subtle, indescribable music.

This experience will reveal something about yourself as a spiritual being. Welcome the change this brings.

Beyond Dreams

The food which is dearest to the chela is that of the words and discourses of the Mahanta, the Living ECK Master. Faith in the Mahanta is the armor of the chela and the attitude of the true and pure seekers of truth. Each loves the things which the world utterly rejects as being impractical and much too dreamlike.

—*SKS*, Bk. 2, p. 215

*B*efore reading from an ECK book or discourse, close your eyes and imagine you are sitting at a dining-room table with the Master. He has laid out a wondrous meal, each dish radiant with the love that went into preparing it.

Take up your fork or spoon, and eat this nourishing, satisfying, and delicious fare to your heart's content. You may catch the twinkle in the Master's eye as you feast.

Come back and read your book.

* * *

In your daily life you may find yourself less concerned when your perceptions differ from those around you. It is a feeling of freedom and protection.

Freedom of Self-Responsibility

Those who believe that a good education will give them greater spiritual progress are working in an illusion. It will help them to find employment, of course, which is good, but as far as helping them to unfold spiritually, it is not worth much. Naturally, employment is needed, for every chela must stand on his own feet and accept his responsibility here in this world and those worlds beyond.

—*SKS*, Bk. 2, p. 216

*A*sk the Mahanta to show you the next spiritual step in self-responsibility. Put this request in writing as a true prayer to the Master. Take your time with it.

He may guide you to a series of small conscious acts or a major undertaking. Whatever the response, it will be right for you.

This will prepare you to take on a greater responsibility you have desired, here and in the inner worlds.

The Source of HU

All true seekers of the Sugmad must find the Living ECK Master and surrender themselves to him, because this is the only way of purifying the mind in this Kali Yuga age. As long as the mind is not purified, there can be no liberation of Soul. Only the Mahanta, the Living ECK Master is familiar with the Ocean of Love and Mercy and can take his disciples to this final region. No one else knows the supreme secrets of the path of ECK. Only by his grace is liberation attained.

—*SKS*, Bk. 2, pp. 216–17

*F*ind a quiet, private place, and shut your eyes. Chant *HU* softly, and let the sound mix with your breath—going out from you like the waves of an ocean, one upon the other.

The Mahanta will lead you to the source of waves, the source of HU.

*   *   *

Observe the Mahanta's grace at work in your life. He will reveal why certain thoughts and actions can be obstacles to unfoldment. This will bring a needed help and healing.

Holy Service

> Those who know the secret of the Living Word and are in the holy service of the ECK are extremely fortunate, for the company and the society of the ECKists in their community as well as that of the Mahanta, the Living ECK Master is precious in this age of the Kali Yuga.
>
> —*SKS*, Bk. 2, p. 218

In contemplation, sing the word *satya* (SAHT-yah), as in the Satya Yuga, meaning golden, twelve times. See the Mahanta plant a golden seed of holy service in your heart. You may see it shimmer with light or pulse with life.

Accept it with love and delight.

*   *   *

Keep your heart open to the Mahanta, and in the natural course of your day, you will have more than one opportunity to rise to the call of service. You may not see it as such at the time, nor guess its purpose.

These are spiritual turning points and can lead you to God.

Training for Mastership

Vanity is the greatest Kal passion which those in training for the ECK Mastership must watch. It is subtle and can reach out putting its claws into the mind and heart of the trainee, and without his knowing it, he practices vanity. Those in training serve their Master with care and happiness. The eyes of the trainee are blessed by looking at the Mahanta, the Living ECK Master.

—*SKS*, Bk. 2, pp. 219–20

*S*ing the word *dinta* softly, sweetly, for several minutes.

Using your Spiritual Eye, look into the face of the Inner Master. You may also use a photo if you choose. Continue to sing *dinta*.

*   *   *

At some point during your day, say to yourself, "I am taking this action in the name of the Mahanta, with all my love and care," and do so, whatever it is.

If your goal is ECK Mastership, this regular practice will serve you well.

The Treasure Map

Whatever is good for each individual is equally good for the Mahanta, the Living ECK Master. Therefore, he never deprives anyone of anything, nor gives to anyone something which is greater than the other. All things are given in proportion to how much the chela can receive.

If it appears that he takes away something in the material world, then he must replace it in another way for that individual with whom he is working to reach perfection.

—SKS, Bk. 2, p. 221

*D*o you feel you have suffered a loss of some kind? Chant *HU* for several minutes and, with your Spiritual Eye, imagine the Mahanta has handed you a treasure map. On it he has marked where to look for what he has replaced your loss with.

* * *

In your outer life, this gift may come through some unlikely door or happening. It may come as a spiritual realization, a change in attitude, or a virtue such as humility.

How much can you receive?

159

Love and Miracles

> The Mahanta, the Living ECK Master does not exhibit miracles; for love is not based upon miracles. Miracles are shown only to true seekers who believe in and love the Mahanta.
>
> —*SKS*, Bk. 2, p. 223

*S*ing *Wah Z* softly, like a whisper to yourself, for a few moments.

The Master knows exactly what miracle will be of the greatest spiritual benefit to you. Fill your heart with pure love, and it will find you.

Remember to look in your dream journal, into the eyes of people and animals, at the small nudges and coincidences throughout your day.

CHAPTER 12

The Circles of ECK Initiations

Radiant Service

The initiation into Eckankar is the true way, and the radiant form of the Mahanta, the Vi-Guru, the Light Giver, lights up every Soul who enters into it, with the sacred word for each, which is personal and secret to everyone who is looking for enlightenment in God.

—*SKS*, Bk. 2, p. 229

*L*ook inwardly for the Light Giver as you chant *Vi-Guru* for several minutes.

The Mahanta's radiant form can be seen, felt, or heard. It can feel like the warmth of the sun or sound like the singing of happy atoms. It can appear as an iridescent constellation of the Master's physical form.

*   *   *

This presence of the Master puts a greater light to Soul. To be aware of this, find a way to be of special service to someone today.

Spiritual Development

> If he does not remember anything about the First Initiation, which was received in the dream state, he has missed a great deal, because there is a deep responsibility which goes with his spiritual development during the time he spends in the First Circle of ECK initiation.
>
> The chela may not realize that he has entered into the heart of life when he has received the First Initiation.
>
> —*SKS*, Bk. 2, p. 231

*W*hat is the heart of life?

This is the Master's question under discussion in a class meeting on the inner planes. Go into contemplation and join them.

This inner experience will reveal at least one answer that lights up your being from the inside out.

You can also ask for a dream to experience the heart of life. The Master will be listening.

Alignment of HU

The mind is incapable of grasping reality; therefore, it is necessary to undertake a course of discipline that enables one to take the path of ECK that will allow the lower emotional and intellectual centers to come into contact with the higher ones.

—*SKS*, Bk. 2, p. 232

*T*ake a few moments to relax and let go of the thoughts of the day.

Begin by singing *HU* with all your love. Visualize your thoughts, attitudes, and opinions aligning with this sacred sound. Let the pure love and power of HU penetrate and purify every thought, every feeling.

*　　*　　*

There will be some event or issue in your day that will benefit from this alignment. But you will need self-discipline to act on it.

The Center Path

> The initiation of the Second Circle is that where the limited consciousness in man comes into the state of decision. This decision is what road shall the chela take: the left-hand path which is that of black magic, the right-hand path which is that of white magic, or the center path which is the road of the purified Soul.
>
> —*SKS*, Bk. 2, p. 233

*W*ith your Spiritual Eye, imagine you are walking along a path which then divides itself three ways. There may appear to be something attractive or enticing on both the right- and left-hand path. However, the Master waits for you on the center path. Walk with Z, and he will speak with you about your choice.

*   *   *

By taking the center path, you will be shown how to make choices based on your goals of Self-Realization and God-Realization.

All possible help will be given in advance of your need for it.

The Active Force of ECK

Perpetual change is the very essence of manifestation, and in that transmutation the medium for
the action of the neutralizing force, by this very
change, now becomes the medium through which
the active force of ECK acts and enters into that Soul
which has selected the middle path for perfection.

—*SKS*, Bk. 2, pp. 234–35

*W*hat do you seek to manifest in your life? Be
thoughtful about this.

Sing the word *Akasha*, a word for the primal matter
force, and see the ECK Itself enter into Soul. Inwardly
present your desire to the Master, heart to heart.

*   *   *

Know that if your desire is of spiritual benefit to
you, the Mahanta will see that you receive ample opportunity to accept the necessary changes.

Follow through to see results.

Soul Untouched

Man's behavior has always been triggered by fear. This knowledge alone about him has been used throughout history to degrade him. But the mechanical man has never been able to recognize the insidious mental degradation of superstitions and the social, pseudoscientific, and pseudoreligious actions which have crippled his mind and left Soul untouched.

—*SKS*, Bk. 2, p. 235

*D*oes fear shadow you?

Sing *HU* or your secret word for several moments. Little by little, see the Light of ECK fill your being, until the shadow of fear is burned away by the brilliance of Soul's own Light.

Let the strength of this Light protectively seal your aura completely. Visualize this using your Spiritual Eye.

*   *   *

Exercise this protection. When fear and self-doubt creep up on you, sing *HU* and fill yourself with the Light of Soul.

Trust and Confidence

Man's perceptions on any concept which is beyond him develops into trust and faith that all will
be well provided. He will leave the ECK alone and
let It work in him to grow into the mighty stream,
which It assuredly will, in time. This is the development of the progressive knowledge of the Sugmad.

—*SKS*, Bk. 2, p. 236

*S*ing the word *santosha* in contemplation for a time.
This is a word for spiritual contentment, one of the
virtues of Soul.

Imagine a river of Light and Sound entering through
the crown chakra, at the top of your head, and flowing
through your being. Feel your body welcome this living
stream of divine love.

*   *   *

Acceptance of the Master's love in this way increas-
es humility, right discrimination, forgiveness, and detachment. Look for evidence of this during your day.

Fire of Soul

The initiation of the Fifth Circle is sometimes known as the transfiguration. This transfiguration takes place when the mind has finally come under control and is balanced with the rest of the personality so that the fire of Soul, and the Light of the plane along with the ECK Sound Current, affects it, reflects upon it, and can permanently illuminate the personality.

—*SKS*, Bk. 2, p. 238

*B*egin by singing *HU* or your secret word.

Imagine meeting the Master outdoors in the evening, under the stars. He is putting a log on the campfire and takes a seat beside you. In the flickering glow of golden light, he begins to speak about the fire of Soul. His words reach your heart.

*   *   *

Think of this firelight during your day, and feel it in your heart. Each time you do this, its glow will light your thoughts and actions with the ECK Current.

Spiritual Flexibility

The initiate has learned that by self-surrender he does not resist life, but goes along with it in an active manner. He is like the willow bough which is weighed down by the winter snow and does not resist but bends spontaneously under the weight so the snow falls off. In his relationship with the Mahanta, the Living ECK Master he accepts all the burdens of life because they will be destroyed by their own weight.

—*SKS*, Bk. 2, p. 240

*S*hut your eyes and chant the word *Shab* for several minutes. It means the lover of life.

Open your Spiritual Eye, and see how this love current brings a supple flexibility to your inner bodies. Experiment with this inwardly. Maybe you become an acrobat, bounce on a trampoline, or dance with joy for life. Give it your all.

* * *

Whenever possible, practice surrender to the Mahanta. It brings the freedom to express your true self in new ways.

One of the Few

From the time the initiate left the circle of the Fourth Initiation, he has been watched carefully by the Adepts of the Vairagi, for he is one of the selected few whom they know will eventually enter into the glorious heights of the Ninth Lok (plane), where his responsibility is exceedingly greater and cannot be shirked.

—*SKS*, Bk. 2, p. 242

*T*his one day, imagine that you are being observed by the Adepts of the Vairagi for greater freedom and responsibility in the worlds. Do this regardless of your present initiation level.

Have no preconception of this exercise.

As you reflect on this throughout your day, certain insights will come to you. They may be very subtle. Note each of these awakenings carefully. They hold keys to your path to Mastership.

A Living Parable

Here it is learned that the ECK is not energy of Itself, but It controls and directs energy in all the worlds of God. That the end product of spiritual evolution by man on earth is by instruction and discipline, and that he must see to it that he is free at all times to follow the Mahanta, the Living ECK Master.

—*SKS*, Bk. 2, pp. 244–45

*I*magine that you are standing on a dock by a large body of water. The Master is in a small boat some distance offshore, and he invites you to join him. How will you do this? Sing Z, and let the experience unfold.

This living parable will show you another step in what it means to be free to follow the Mahanta at all times.

Enjoy your story!

A Light of the World

Every initiate in ECK is linked up with the ECK, the Audible Life Stream, and is an added force for the whole movement of Eckankar. Therefore, he becomes a channel of his own under the Living ECK Master, and his responsibilities should never be lightly taken for each initiate is a potential light of the world.

—*SKS*, Bk. 2, p. 247

*O*pen *The Shariyat*, and read about the four ECK margs on pages 246–47.

The Inner Master will help you choose one of the four orders to focus on—Arahata, Bhakti, Giani, or Vahana. For ten to twenty minutes, chant the word for the marg you chose. Or you can chant each word for five minutes or so.

Open your heart to receive the divine action of the Sound Current. This blessing will refine the direction of your life.

*   *   *

In this lifetime, you can find a depth of purpose—heights of fulfillment and joy—beyond anything you could imagine.

Begin with one simple act of love in the name of the Sugmad.

The world is waiting.

About the Author

Author Harold Klemp is known as a pioneer of today's focus on "everyday spirituality." He was raised on a Wisconsin farm and attended divinity school. He also served in the US Air Force.

In 1981, after lifetimes of training, he became the spiritual leader of Eckankar, the Path of Spiritual Freedom. His full title is Sri Harold Klemp, the Mahanta, the Living ECK Master. His mission is to help people find their way back to God in this life.

Each year, Harold Klemp speaks to thousands of seekers at Eckankar seminars. Author of more than one hundred books, he continues to write, including many articles and spiritual-study discourses. His inspiring and practical approach to spirituality helps many thousands of people worldwide find greater freedom, wisdom, and love in their lives.

For Further Reading and Study

Spiritual Exercises for the Shariyat, Book One
Harold Klemp

Spiritual gold awaits your discovery in these spiritual exercises. The Master offers you a personal invitation to experience the Shariyat on the inner planes in his company. Try a new technique to resolve karmic debts, and find healing and joy where you might never think to look. Infinite opportunities for growth and wonder are at your fingertips.

The Shariyat-Ki-Sugmad
Book One

Through *The Shariyat-Ki-Sugmad* you will discover an answer to every human question ever yet, or to be, devised. Its pages tell what life really consists of and how to live it. Book One is the first section of these works, which was dictated by Fubbi Quantz, the great ECK Master.

The Shariyat-Ki-Sugmad
Book Two

Book Two is the second section of these sacred writings from the Temples of Golden Wisdom in the spiritual worlds. It was dictated by Yaubl Sacabi, the great ECK Master. The essence of God-knowledge is laid down here.

The Shariyat-Ki-Sugmad
Books One & Two
The special one-volume edition with a combined index is bound in soft, blue leather; the pages are gilt-edged and carefully stitched.

The Shariyat-Ki-Sugmad, Book One
Audiobook (CD)
The Shariyat-Ki-Sugmad, which means "Way of the Eternal," is the holy scripture of Eckankar. Enjoy listening to the ancient scriptures of God's love for you.

The Shariyat-Ki-Sugmad, Book Two
Audiobook (CD)
Deepen your understanding of Soul and Its service to God in this second book of Eckankar's holy scriptures.

The Spiritual Exercises of ECK
Harold Klemp
This book is a staircase with 131 steps leading to the doorway to spiritual freedom, self-mastery, wisdom, and love. A comprehensive volume of spiritual exercises for every need.

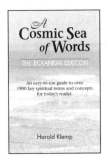

A Cosmic Sea of Words: The ECKANKAR Lexicon
Harold Klemp

The ultimate companion book for all Eckankar literature. An easy-to-use guide to over 1,900 key spiritual terms and concepts for today's reader.

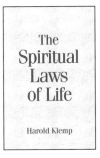

The Spiritual Laws of Life
Harold Klemp

Learn how to keep in tune with your true spiritual nature. Spiritual laws reveal the behind-the-scenes forces at work in your daily life.

179

Advanced Spiritual Living

Go higher, further, deeper with your spiritual exploration!

ECK membership brings many unique benefits and a focus on the ECK discourses. These are dynamic spiritual courses you study at home, one per month.

The first year of study brings *The Easy Way Discourses* by Harold Klemp, with uplifting spiritual exercises, audio excerpts from his seminar talks, and activities to 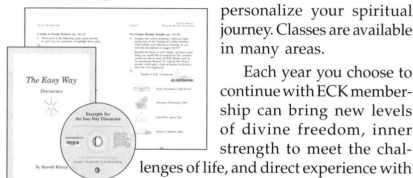 personalize your spiritual journey. Classes are available in many areas.

Each year you choose to continue with ECK membership can bring new levels of divine freedom, inner strength to meet the challenges of life, and direct experience with the love and power of God.

Here's a sampling of titles from *The Easy Way Discourses*:

- In Soul You Are Free
- Reincarnation—Why You Came to Earth Again
- The Master Principle
- The God Worlds—Where No One Has Gone Before?

How to Get Started

For free books and more information about Eckankar:

- Visit www.Eckankar.org;
- Call 1-800-LOVE GOD (1-800-568-3463), ext. BK 151 (USA and Canada only); or

- Write to: ECKANKAR, Dept. BK 151, PO Box 2000, Chanhassen, MN 55317-2000 USA.

To order Eckankar books online, you can visit www.ECKBooks.org.

To receive your advanced spiritual-study discourses, along with other annual membership benefits, go to www.Eckankar.org (click on "Membership" then "Online Membership Application"). You can also call Eckankar at (952) 380-2222 to apply. Or write to the address above, Att: Membership.